Top 100 A Recipes

Published by Alexey Evdokimov

Copyright 2016 Alexey Evdokimov

Black and white version of the book

Table of Contents:

Top 100 Amazing Parfait Recipes 1
    Introduction 5
    What is a Parfait ? 6
1. Caramel Apple Yogurt Parfaits 7
2. Sky Parfaits 8
3. Strawberry-Banana Lactose Free Parfaits 9
4. Mango-Coconut Parfaits 10
5. Angel-Fruit Parfaits 11
6. Lemon Angel Parfaits 12
7. Mexican Chocolate-Raspberry Parfaits 13
8. Gluten-Free Cookie, Greek Yogurt and Fruit Parfaits 14
9. Halloween Snake-Bite Parfaits 15
10. Mixed-Berry Butter Crunch Parfaits 16
11. Mint Brownie Parfaits 17
12. Fruit Parfaits 18
13. Red, White and Blue Parfait 19
14. Fiber One Chocolate and Peanut Butter Parfaits 20
15. Strawberry Margarita Parfaits 21
16. Quinoa Granola Parfaits 22
17. Cottage Cheese Parfait 23

18. Walnut-Yogurt Parfait 24

19. Apricot-Compote Yogurt Parfaits 25

20. Papaya-Berry Yogurt Parfaits 26

21. Watermelon and Coconut Sorbet Parfaits 27

22. Pineapple-Red Quinoa Parfait 28

23. Carrot-Cake Parfaits 29

24. Strawberry Pudding Parfait 30

25. Raspberry Lemonade Cheesecake Parfaits 31

26. Triple Berry Sauce and Triple Berry Parfait 32

27. Easy Greek Yogurt Parfaits 33

28. Chocolate-Raspberry Frozen Yogurt Parfaits 34

29. White Chocolate-Strawberry Yogurt Parfaits 35

30. Kiwi-Pineapple Yogurt Parfaits 36

31. Crunchy Banana-Strawberry Parfaits 37

32. Key Lime Parfaits 38

33. End-Of-The-Rainbow Cookie Parfaits 39

34. Monster Cereal Pudding Parfaits 40

35. Easy Pumpkin and Fudge Parfaits 41

36. Poison Apple Parfaits 42

37. Plum Pudding Parfaits 43

38. Ambrosia Yogurt Parfaits 44

39. Berry Brownie Parfaits 45

40. Sun and Sky Yogurt Parfait 46

41. Cranberry Parfaits 47

42. Raspberry-Cookie Parfaits 48

43. Raspberry Lemon Dessert Yogurt Parfaits 49

44. Chocolate Crunch Cheesecake Parfait 50

45. Chocolate-Kiwi-Berry Parfaits 51

46. Fudgy-Peanut Butter Banana Parfaits 52

47. Patriotic Parfaits 53

48. Praline Peach Parfaits 54

49. Fresh Strawberry and Rhubarb Sauce Parfaits 55

50. Frosted Toast Crunch Berry Parfaits 56

51. Trix Very Berry Parfaits 57

52. Pumpkin Parfaits 58

53. Coconut Pumpkin Parfaits 59

54. Blueberry Trifle Parfaits 60

55. Homemade Eggnog Ice Cream Parfaits 61

56. Healthified Tiramisu Parfaits 62

57. Creamy Caramel-Peach Parfaits 63

58. Vanilla Cupcakes, Blueberry And Whipped Topping Jar Parfaits.......64

59. Neapolitan Shortcake Parfaits 65

60. Chocolate-Banana Pudding Parfaits 67

61. Tiramisu With Cookie Crisp 68

62. Peanut Butter Cheerios Pudding Carnival..69

63. Luscious Lemon Bar Parfait...70

64. Apple Cinnamon Parfait...71

65. Butterscotch Mousse Parfait 72

66. St. Patrick's Day Parfait...73

67. Key Lime Pie Parfait..74

68. Red Velvet Parfaits 75

69. Black-Bottom Strawberry Cream Parfaits...76

70. Crunchy-Topped Strawberry-Kiwi Parfaits 77

71. Mango Parfait..78

72. Vanilla & Mocha Parfaits Mini's..79

73. Cherry and Amaretti Parfaits 80

74. Gingersnap and Jam Parfaits ... 81
75. Emeril's Late-Night Parfaits ... 82
76. Savory Tomato Parfaits ... 83
77. Mango & Raspberry Parfait ... 84
78. Banana Chai Smoothie Parfait ... 86
79. Strawberry Frozen Yogurt Parfaits ... 87
80. Easy Breakfast Parfait ... 88
81. Twix Trifles ... 89
82. Roasted Cherry Parfait ... 91
83. Roasted Peach Parfaits ... 92
84. Vanilla Bean Yogurt and Nectarine Parfait With Candied Nuts ... 93
85. Cool & Creamy Oreo Parfaits ... 94
86. Grasshopper Parfaits ... 95
87. Carrot Cake Parfaits ... 96
88. Snickers Pudding Parfaits ... 98
89. Lemon Mascarpone Parfaits ... 99
90. Cinnamon Apple Pear Parfait ... 100
91. Banana Coconut Cream Pie Parfaits ... 101
92. Special K Parfait ... 103
93. Mother's Day Spring Parfait ... 104
94. Amaranth Yogurt Parfait ... 106
95. Sweet and Toasty Parfait ... 107
96. Walnut Ginger Granola Parfait ... 108
97. Tropical "Candy Corn" Protein Parfait ... 109
98. Spiked Peppermint Brownie Parfait ... 110
99. Rainbow Dessert Parfaits ... 111
100. Sweetheart Strawberry Yogurt Parfaits ... 112

Introduction

Considering the fact that the parfait is such an amazing dessert, you wouldn't be surprised that "parfait" in French means perfect. The parfait is usually served in small cups, it's creamy and there are lot of flavors to try. It's an ideal dessert to serve after lunch or even when hosting parties. If you never tried making them by yourself, or you did and they were so great that you have to make again, here are 100 recipes to check out. They all are very tasty and there are flavors to satisfy everyone's preferences. Bon Appetit!

What is a Parfait?

Parfait (from French meaning "perfect") is a kind of frozen dessert that dates to 1894. In France, parfait refers to a frozen dessert made from a base of sugar syrup, egg, and cream. A parfait contains enough fat, sugar, alcohol, and/or, to a lesser extent, air to allow it to be made by stirring infrequently while freezing, making it possible to create in a home kitchen without specialist equipment. The fat, sugar, alcohol or air interferes with the formation of water crystals, which would otherwise give the ice cream an uncomfortable texture in the mouth. The formation of ice crystals is managed in the making of regular ice cream by agitating the ice cream constantly while it freezes or chemically by adding glycerol. Neither should be necessary when making a high-quality parfait.

In the United States, parfait refers to either the traditional French-style dessert or to a popular variant, the American parfait, made by layering parfait cream, ice cream, and/or flavored gelatins in a tall, clear glass, and topping the creation with whipped cream, fresh or canned fruit, and/or liqueurs.

In Canada and the United States, parfaits may also be made by using yogurt layered with granola, nuts or fresh fruits, such as peaches, strawberries, or blueberries.

1. Caramel Apple Yogurt Parfaits

Enjoy this delicious parfait layered with fat free yogurt, apples and caramel topping that is ready in 10 minutes – perfect for a dessert.

INGREDIENTS

- ✓ 2 cups fat free creamy vanilla yogurt or fat free plain yogurt (from 2-lb container)
- ✓ 2 medium unpeeled apples or pears, cut into chunks (2 cups)
- ✓ 1/4 cup caramel fat-free topping
- ✓ 2 tablespoons coarsely chopped pecans or walnuts

INSTRUCTIONS

1) Reserve 1/4 cup yogurt for topping. Divide remaining yogurt among 4 (8-oz) glasses or dessert dishes. Spoon 1/2 cup of the apple chunks over yogurt in each glass.

2) Top each with 1 tablespoon of the remaining yogurt. Spoon 1 tablespoon caramel topping over yogurt. Sprinkle pecans over each parfait. Serve immediately.

2. Sky Parfaits

These easy, adorable gelatin parfaits are sure to generate smiles!

INGREDIENTS

- ✓ 1 (3 ounce) package blue gelatin
- ✓ 1 cup whipped topping

INSTRUCTIONS

1) Prepare the gelatin per box instructions. Refrigerate until fully set.
2) Rake set gelatin with a fork to form globules.
3) Layer in parfait glasses, alternating with whipped topping to form clouds and sky.
4) Enjoy!!!

3. Strawberry-Banana Lactose Free Parfaits

You're 5 ingredients away from dipping into a delicious, layered yogurt, fruit and cereal parfait.

INGREDIENTS

- ✓ 2 containers (6 oz each) Lactose Free strawberry yogurt
- ✓ 2 cups Fiber One Honey Cluster cereal
- ✓ 1 cup sliced fresh strawberries
- ✓ 1 medium banana, thinly sliced
- ✓ 4 whole fresh strawberries

INSTRUCTIONS

1) In each of 4 (10 oz) parfait glasses, layer 2 tablespoons yogurt, 1/4 cup cereal, 1/4 cup strawberry slices and 1/4 of the banana slices.

2) Top each parfait with 2 tablespoons yogurt, 1/4 cup cereal and remaining yogurt. Garnish with whole strawberry.

4. Mango-Coconut Parfaits

Layer cake, mango, coconut and whipped cream to make this wonderful parfait - a wonderful dessert.

INGREDIENTS

- ✓ 4 cups cubed pound cake
- ✓ 1 1/2 cups whipping cream
- ✓ 1/4 cup canned cream of coconut (not coconut milk)
- ✓ 2 tablespoons powdered sugar
- ✓ 3/4 cup canned coconut milk (not cream of coconut)
- ✓ 3 cups cubed peeled mangoes
- ✓ 1/2 cup sweetened flaked coconut, toasted

INSTRUCTIONS

1) Heat oven to 350°F. Spread cake cubes in even layer in ungreased 15x10x1-inch pan. Bake 15 to 20 minutes, stirring once, until toasted. Cool completely.
2) In chilled medium bowl, beat whipping cream, cream of coconut and powdered sugar with electric mixer on high speed until soft peaks form.
3) In 6 parfait glasses or dessert dishes, place half of the cake cubes. Spoon 1 tablespoon coconut milk over cake cubes in each glass. Top evenly with half of the mangoes and half of the whipped cream. Sprinkle each with 2 teaspoons toasted coconut. Repeat layers. Serve or refrigerate.

5. Angel-Fruit Parfaits

Serve up refreshing fresh fruit with angel food cake and yogurt. The layering makes it impressive.

INGREDIENTS

- ✓ 1 cup cubed angel food cake
- ✓ 1/2 cup quartered fresh strawberries
- ✓ 1/2 cup cubed peeled mango
- ✓ 1/2 cup cubed cantaloupe or honeydew melon
- ✓ 1/2 medium banana, sliced
- ✓ 2/3 cup Fat Free creamy vanilla yogurt (from 2-lb container)
- ✓ 2 tablespoons sliced almonds, toasted

INSTRUCTIONS

1) In 2 parfait glasses or dessert bowls, alternate layers of cake, fruit, yogurt and almonds.

2) Top each serving with almonds. Serve immediately.

6. Lemon Angel Parfaits

Looking for a beautiful dessert? Then check out these lemon flavored parfaits made using coconut, raspberries and angel food cake - a delicious fluffy delight!

INGREDIENTS

- ✓ 1/2 cup flaked coconut
- ✓ 1 (14 to 16-oz.) loaf angel food cake
- ✓ 1 (10-oz.) jar lemon curd
- ✓ 1 pint (2 cups) whipping cream
- ✓ Fresh raspberries, if desired
- ✓ Lemon strips, if desired

INSTRUCTIONS

1) Heat coconut in medium skillet over medium heat until lightly toasted, stirring frequently. Cool 5 minutes or until completely cooled.
2) Using serrated knife; cut cake into 4 equal lengthwise slices. Reserve 1/4 cup lemon curd. Spread cut side of 2 cake slices with remaining lemon curd. Top each with 1 plain slice. Cut sandwiched slices into 3/4-inch pieces.
3) In medium bowl, beat reserved 1/4 cup lemon curd and whipping cream until stiff peaks form.
4) Place half of cake pieces in 8 parfait or tall stemmed glasses. Top each with 1/4 cup cream mixture and about 1/2 tablespoon toasted coconut. Repeat with remaining cake, cream and coconut. Refrigerate at least 2 hours or until serving time. Garnish with raspberries and lemon strips.

7. Mexican Chocolate-Raspberry Parfaits

Dessert for two? Whip up a delicious soymilk parfait in just 15 minutes.

INGREDIENTS

- 1 1/4 cups light chocolate soymilk
- 1 box (4-serving size) chocolate instant pudding and pie filling mix
- 1/4 teaspoon ground cinnamon
- 1 slice (4x1 inch) angel food cake, torn into pieces
- 1/2 cup frozen (thawed) fat-free whipped topping
- 1/2 cup fresh or frozen (thawed and drained) raspberries
- Grated semisweet chocolate, if desired

INSTRUCTIONS

1) In medium bowl, beat soymilk, pudding mix and cinnamon with wire whisk until mixture is blended and thickened.

2) To assemble, spoon 1/4 cup pudding into each of 2 small parfait glasses or clear drinking glasses. Layer each with half of the cake, 2 tablespoons whipped topping and half of the raspberries. Top each with remaining pudding and whipped topping. Garnish with grated chocolate.

8. Gluten-Free Cookie, Greek Yogurt and Fruit Parfaits

Treat your family to these delicious yogurt, cookie and fruit layered parfaits!

INGREDIENTS

- ✓ 6 tablespoons Pillsbury Gluten Free refrigerated chocolate chip cookie dough (from 14.3-oz container)
- ✓ 2 cups Yoplait Greek 100 plain yogurt (from 2-lb container)
- ✓ 1 tablespoon agave syrup or honey
- ✓ 1 medium mango, coarsely chopped (3/4 cup)
- ✓ 1 medium nectarine, coarsely chopped (3/4 cup)
- ✓ 6 strawberries, sliced
- ✓ 1/2 cup blueberries
- ✓ 2 tablespoons unsweetened coconut chips or shredded coconut (optional)

INSTRUCTIONS

1) Bake 6 cookies as directed on cookie dough container. Cool completely, about 30 minutes. Coarsely crumble cookies.
2) In medium bowl, mix yogurt with agave syrup to sweeten. In another medium bowl, mix mango, nectarine, strawberries and blueberries.
3) In 4 decorative glasses, begin layering yogurt mixture, cookies, fruit, and repeat the layering once more for 2 layers. Put a small dollop of yogurt on top, and sprinkle with coconut.

9. Halloween Snake-Bite Parfaits

These fruity parfaits, made fast with flavored gelatin, yogurt, and frozen fruit, have a deliciously wicked bit of heat.

INGREDIENTS

- ✓ 1 box (4-serving size) strawberry-flavored gelatin
- ✓ 1/2 to 1/4 teaspoon ground red pepper (cayenne)
- ✓ 3/4 cup boiling water
- ✓ 1 box (10 oz) frozen strawberries in light syrup, thawed
- ✓ 1 package (8 oz) cream cheese, softened
- ✓ 2 tablespoons sugar
- ✓ 1 container (6 oz) Fat Free French vanilla yogurt
- ✓ 1/2 teaspoon vanilla

INSTRUCTIONS

1) In small bowl, mix gelatin and red pepper. Pour boiling water on gelatin; stir until gelatin is dissolved. Stir in strawberries in syrup. Refrigerate 15 minutes; stir. If not thickened, refrigerate about 15 minutes longer or until thickened but not firm.
2) In large bowl, beat cream cheese and sugar with electric mixer on low speed until blended. Add yogurt and vanilla; beat until blended. Scoop rounded tablespoonful in each of 8 (4- to 5-oz) liquor glasses or plastic cups. DO NOT LEVEL OUT.
3) Spoon 2 tablespoons strawberry mixture over cream cheese mixture on each. DO NOT LEVEL OUT. Top each with rounded tablespoonful cream cheese mixture, then strawberry mixture.

10. Mixed-Berry Butter Crunch Parfaits

INGREDIENTS

- 1 cup Gold Medal all-purpose flour
- 1/2 cup packed brown sugar
- 1/3 cup coarsely chopped pecans or walnuts
- 1/2 cup cold butter or margarine
- 1 1/2 cups Fiber One cereal
- 1/3 cup flaked coconut
- 6 containers (6 oz each) Fat Free red raspberry yogurt
- 1 1/2 cups blackberries, blueberries and raspberries

INSTRUCTIONS

1) Heat oven to 400°F. In large bowl, mix flour, brown sugar and pecans. Cut in butter, using pastry blender (or pulling 2 table knives through ingredients in opposite directions), until mixture is crumbly. Stir in cereal and coconut. Spread in ungreased 13x9-inch pan.

2) Bake 15 minutes, stirring once. Remove from oven; stir and cool 10 to 15 minutes.

3) In each of 6 parfait glasses, layer 1 to 2 tablespoons cereal mixture, 1/2 container of yogurt and 2 tablespoons berries; repeat layers. Top each with 1 tablespoon cereal mixture. If desired, garnish with additional berries. Store remaining cereal mixture in refrigerator.

11. Mint Brownie Parfaits

INGREDIENTS

- ✓ 1 box (1 lb 2.4 oz) Betty Crocker Original Supreme Premium brownie mix
- ✓ Water, vegetable oil and egg called for on brownie mix box
- ✓ 15 thin rectangular crème de menthe chocolate candies, unwrapped, very coarsely chopped (1/2 cup)
- ✓ 1/2 cup whipping cream
- ✓ 1 tablespoon powdered or granulated sugar
- ✓ 1/8 teaspoon mint extract
- ✓ 1 quart (4 cups) mint chocolate chip ice cream
- ✓ 8 maraschino cherries with stems

INSTRUCTIONS

1) Heat oven to 350°F. Spray 9-inch square pan with cooking spray. Make brownie mix as directed on box, using water, oil and egg and adding chocolate candies. Pour batter into pan.

2) Bake 34 to 37 minutes or until toothpick inserted 2 inches from side of pan comes out almost clean. Cool in pan on cooling rack 30 minutes. Cut into 4 rows by 4 rows. Reserve 8 brownies for another use; cut remaining 8 brownies in half.

3) In chilled medium bowl, beat whipping cream, sugar and mint extract with electric mixer on low speed until mixture begins to thicken. Gradually increase speed to high and beat until soft peaks form.

4) To serve, in each of 8 parfait glasses, layer 1/4 cup ice cream, 1 brownie half and 1 tablespoon whipped cream. Repeat layers once. Top each parfait with 1 cherry.

12. Fruit Parfaits

Five ingredients and less than 10 minutes is all you'll need to wrap up dessert made using fruits topped with almonds.

INGREDIENTS

- ✓ 1/2 cup chopped cantaloupe
- ✓ 1/2 cup sliced strawberries
- ✓ 1/2 cup sliced kiwifruit or honeydew melon
- ✓ 1/2 banana, sliced
- ✓ 1 cup vanilla artificially sweetened low-fat yogurt
- ✓ 2 tablespoons sliced almonds, toasted

INSTRUCTIONS

1) Alternate layers of fruit and yogurt in 2 goblets or parfait glasses, beginning and ending with fruit.
2) Top with almonds.

13. Red, White and Blue Parfait

INGREDIENTS

- ✓ 8 ounces fresh strawberries (for about 1 C chopped)
- ✓ 1/4 cup sugar
- ✓ 4 ounces store-bought pecan sandies, see note (about 8 cookies, for 1 C crumbs)
- ✓ 1/2 cup Cool Whip Lite
- ✓ 4 teaspoons Cool Whip Lite (to garnish)
- ✓ 1/2 cup low-fat vanilla yogurt
- ✓ 8 ounces about 1 c fresh blueberries

INSTRUCTIONS

1) Cap strawberries, cut into bite-size pieces and place them in small mixing bowl.
2) Sprinkle sugar over berries and stir. Use spoon to crush berries slightly so they will release juice. Set aside.
3) Place cookies in zipper-top plastic bag and use rolling pin to crush them finely. Set aside.
4) In small bowl or 2-cup measure, stir together 1/2 C of whipped topping and yogurt until well blended. Set aside.
5) Divide cookie crumbs evenly in bottom of 4 parfait glasses or other dessert dishes (that hold at least 1 cup).

6) Spoon strawberry mixture evenly over crumbs.
7) Spoon yogurt mixture evenly over strawberries.
8) Divide blueberries evenly, and scatter them over yogurt mixture in each dish.
9) The dishes may be served at once or covered with plastic wrap and refrigerated until ready to serve, up to 3 hours.
10) Just before serving, dollop 1 tsp of whipped topping on top of each dish as a garnish.
11) Note: Plain shortbread cookies, vanilla wafers or butter cookies may be substituted for the pecan sandies.

14. Fiber One Chocolate and Peanut Butter Parfaits

INGREDIENTS

- ✓ 1 1/2 cups chocolate pudding
- ✓ 1 cup creamy peanut butter
- ✓ 1 cup whipped cream
- ✓ 1 box Fiber One 90 Calorie Bar (any flavor)

INSTRUCTIONS

1) Layer chocolate, peanut butter, and crumbled Fiber One in a parfait glass and top with whipped cream. Garnish with crumbled Fiber One and serve!

15. Strawberry Margarita Parfaits

Wave your sombrero and have some fun with this pretty layered dessert, with fruity flavors and a spirited (and optional) tequila kick.

INGREDIENTS

- 1/4 cup fresh lime juice
- 2 tablespoons orange juice
- 1 teaspoon unflavored gelatin
- 1 tablespoon tequila
- 1 tablespoon orange-flavored liqueur
- 2 teaspoons grated lime peel
- 1 (14-oz.) can sweetened condensed milk
- 1 cup whipping cream, whipped
- 1 quart (4 cups) fresh strawberries, sliced

INSTRUCTIONS

1) In medium saucepan, combine lime juice and orange juice. Sprinkle gelatin over top; let stand 1 minute to soften. Heat over low heat until clear and dissolved, stirring occasionally. Cool 5 minutes.
2) Add tequila, liqueur, lime peel and condensed milk to gelatin mixture; mix well. Fold in whipped cream.
3) Divide one-third of the strawberries among individual 10-oz. parfait glasses. Top with half of the tequila mixture. Top with half of the remaining strawberries and all of the remaining tequila mixture. Top with remaining strawberries. Cover glasses with plastic wrap; refrigerate at least 2 hours before serving.

16. Quinoa Granola Parfaits

Quinoa adds extra crunch and nutrients to this crunchy, tasty granola recipe!

INGREDIENTS

- ✓ 2 cups old-fashioned oats
- ✓ 1 cup quinoa (uncooked)
- ✓ 1 cup slivered or roughly-chopped almonds
- ✓ 1/4 cup honey
- ✓ 2 Tbsp. melted coconut oil
- ✓ 1 tsp. salt
- ✓ 1 tsp. ground cinnamon
- ✓ 1 cup shaved coconut (or 2/3 cup grated coconut)
- ✓ 6 oz. dried apricots
- ✓ 6 oz. dried cherries or cranberries

INSTRUCTIONS

1) Preheat oven to 350 degrees.
2) In a large bowl, stir together oats, quinoa, almonds, honey, coconut oil, salt and cinnamon until combined. Spread the mixture out on a foil- or parchment-lined baking sheet. Bake for about 20 minutes, stirring once halfway. Remove sheet and sprinkle the shaved coconut evenly over the top of the granola. Bake for an additional 3-5 minutes (watch closely) until the coconut is toasted. Remove and let cool, then stir in dried fruit and toss to combine.
3) Serve immediately or store in a sealed container for up to 2 weeks.

17. Cottage Cheese Parfait

INGREDIENTS

- 1 navel orange
- 1/2 cup whipped low-fat cottage cheese
- 1/2 cup raspberries
- 1 piece whole-wheat toast

INSTRUCTIONS

1) With a sharp knife, slice off both ends of orange. Following the curve of the fruit, cut away peel and white pith. Halve orange from top to bottom; thinly slice crosswise. Pile half the orange slices and half the raspberries in the bottom of a glass or bowl. Top with cottage cheese, then remaining orange slices and raspberries. Serve with toast.

18. Walnut-Yogurt Parfait

INGREDIENTS

- ✓ 2 cups nonfat Greek yogurt
- ✓ 1 cup fresh fruit (berries, kiwi, oranges)
- ✓ 1/2 cup chopped, toasted walnuts
- ✓ 1 tablespoon honey

INSTRUCTIONS

1) Divide yogurt, fruit, and walnuts between two glasses. Drizzle each with 1/2 tablespoon honey.

19. Apricot-Compote Yogurt Parfaits

INGREDIENTS

- 1/4 cup plus 2 tablespoons honey
- 3 tablespoons water
- Pinch of coarse salt
- 1 pound fresh apricots (5 to 6), pitted and cut into eighths
- 2 containers (17 ounces each) fat-free plain Greek yogurt
- Toasted sliced almonds, for serving (optional)

INSTRUCTIONS

1) In a small saucepan, bring 1/4 cup honey, water, and salt to a simmer over medium; stir until honey dissolves, 1 minute. Add apricots. Raise heat to medium-high and simmer, stirring often, until fruit is soft and liquid is syrupy, 10 to 12 minutes (adjust heat if necessary to keep at a constant simmer). Divide compote among seven small glass jars or airtight containers. Refrigerate, uncovered, until cool, 10 minutes. Stir 1 tablespoon honey into each of the containers of yogurt; divide yogurt among jars. Serve with toasted sliced almonds if desired.

20. Papaya-Berry Yogurt Parfaits

INGREDIENTS

- ✓ 3 containers (5.3 ounces each) plain nonfat Greek yogurt
- ✓ 5 tablespoons honey
- ✓ 1 1/2 teaspoons grated lemon zest, plus 1 tablespoon juice
- ✓ 1 piece fresh ginger (about 2 inches)
- ✓ 1 papaya (1 pound), peeled, halved lengthwise, seeds discarded, cut into 1/2-inch cubes
- ✓ 1 package (6 ounces) fresh blackberries
- ✓ 1 package (6 ounces) fresh raspberries
- ✓ 1/4 cup chopped fresh mint, plus sprigs for garnish
- ✓ 1/2 cup granola

INSTRUCTIONS

1) In a small bowl combine yogurt, 3 tablespoons honey, and zest; set aside.
2) Using the large holes of a box grater, grate the ginger (no need to peel) into a small bowl. Squeeze ginger through a fine-meshed sieve or strainer placed over a medium bowl to get a total of 1 tablespoon ginger juice. Discard pulp. To the bowl with the juice, add remaining 2 tablespoons honey and lemon juice; whisk to combine. Add papaya, blackberries, and raspberries and toss gently to coat.

3) To serve: Spoon half the fruit and juices among six 8-ounce tall glasses. Sprinkle chopped mint over the fruit. Top with half the yogurt mixture and half the granola. Layer with the remaining fruit, yogurt, and granola. Garnish with mint sprigs.

21. Watermelon and Coconut Sorbet Parfaits

INGREDIENTS

- 1/4 cup coconut flakes
- 2 pints store-bought coconut sorbet
- 2 cups cubed (1/2 inch) watermelon
- Finely grated lime zest, for sprinkling

INSTRUCTIONS

1) Preheat oven to 375 degrees. Bake coconut flakes in a single layer on a rimmed baking sheet until toasted, about 3 minutes.

2) Divide half the sorbet among 6 tall glasses using a 2 1/4-inch ice cream scoop. Top each with a layer of watermelon, another scoop of sorbet, and then more watermelon. Sprinkle with lime zest and toasted coconut.

22. Pineapple-Red Quinoa Parfait

INGREDIENTS

- 1/2 teaspoon ground cinnamon
- 6 ounces plain fat-free Greek or soy yogurt, preferably organic
- 1 cup fresh pineapple, cut into chunks
- 1/2 cup cooked red quinoa, chilled
- 2 tablespoons sliced almonds

INSTRUCTIONS

1) Fold cinnamon into yogurt. In a dish, alternately layer pineapple, quinoa, and yogurt; garnish with almonds and serve.

23. Carrot-Cake Parfaits

INGREDIENTS

- ✓ Vegetable-oil cooking spray 8 ounces carrots, peeled and grated (about 4 cups)
- ✓ 2 large eggs
- ✓ 1/2 cup sugar
- ✓ 1/2 cup packed light-brown sugar
- ✓ 1 cup safflower oil
- ✓ 1 tablespoon grated peeled fresh ginger
- ✓ 1 1/2 cups all-purpose flour
- ✓ 1/2 teaspoon baking powder
- ✓ 1/2 teaspoon baking soda
- ✓ 1/2 teaspoon coarse salt
- ✓ 1 teaspoon ground cinnamon
- ✓ 1 teaspoon ground ginger
- ✓ 1 cup apricot jam

INSTRUCTIONS

1) Preheat oven to 350 degrees. Coat a 12 1/2-by-17 1/2-inch rimmed baking sheet with cooking spray. Line with parchment; spray parchment. Whisk together carrots, eggs, sugars, oil, and fresh ginger. In another bowl, whisk together flour, baking powder, baking soda, salt, cinnamon, and ground ginger. Fold flour mixture into carrot mixture.

2) Spread batter in pan. Bake until golden and a toothpick comes out clean, about 20 minutes. Let cool in pan on a wire rack 20 minutes. Invert onto rack; let cool completely. Cut out 16 cake rounds to fit in an 8-to-10-ounce glass, piecing together scraps as necessary.

3) Spoon 2 tablespoons jam into each glass; layer with 1/4 cup filling, then 2 cake rounds, pressing to compact. Top each with 2 tablespoons filling and serve.

24. Strawberry Pudding Parfait

INGREDIENTS

- ✓ 2 small boxes instant strawberry pudding (plus milk to prepare)
- ✓ 2 small boxes instant vanilla pudding (plus milk to prepare)
- ✓ 1 box white cake mix (plus eggs, oil, and water)
- ✓ strawberries, sliced

INSTRUCTIONS

1) Bake cake per package directions. Let cool completely. Cut into small cubes.
2) Prepare puddings per package directions.
3) Beginning and ending with pudding, layer all of the ingredients into a large trifle dish or into individual parfait glasses. Garnish with a strawberry on top.

25. Raspberry Lemonade Cheesecake Parfaits

INGREDIENTS

- 18 ounce fresh raspberries
- 9 graham crackers, crushed
- ½ cup light brown sugar
- ½ cup chopped almonds, finely chopped
- pinch of salt
- ½ cup butter, melted
- 24 ounces cream cheese, softened
- ¾ cup sugar
- 1½ cup frozen whipped topping, thawed
- 21 oz Lucky Leaf Lemon Pie Filling

INSTRUCTIONS

1) Mix crushed graham crackers, brown sugar, chopped almonds, pinch of salt, and melted butter in a bowl. Set aside.

2) In a mixer, blend cream cheese, and sugar until fluffy.

3) Gently fold in thawed whipped topping and lemon pie filling.

4) Layer parfaits in a mason jar starting with graham cracker crust, fresh raspberries, lemon cheesecake filling and repeat layers.

5) Top with whipped cream if desired. Enjoy!

26. Triple Berry Sauce and Triple Berry Parfait

INGREDIENTS

- ✓ 2 cups berries (strawberries, blackberries, and blueberries), cleaned
- ✓ 2 tablespoons water
- ✓ 2 tablespoons butter
- ✓ 2 tablespoons sugar
- ✓ 2 teaspoons cornstarch
- ✓ Triple Berry Sauce
- ✓ Greek Yogurt

INSTRUCTIONS

1) Add fruit to a medium saucepan or skillet over medium heat. Add all other ingredients and bring to a boil for about three minutes. Stir occasionally, reduce heat to low and allow to simmer for about two to three more minutes.

2) Remove from heat and serve warm or store in an airtight container until ready to serve. Then, warm slightly before serving.

3) Layer ½ Greek Yogurt into the bottom of glass to about ½ - 1 inch thickness. Top with equal thickness Triple Berry Sauce. Repeat layers ending with Triple Berry Sauce.

4) Serve cold.

27. Easy Greek Yogurt Parfaits

INGREDIENTS

- Greek yogurt (I used low-fat plain Chobani)
- fresh chopped fruit (any will work!)
- toasted coconut
- pistachios
- chia seeds
- honey

INSTRUCTIONS

1) Place Greek yogurt in a bowl (or keep in container). Top with fruit, coconut, pistachios, chia seeds, then drizzle with honey. Enjoy!

28. Chocolate-Raspberry Frozen Yogurt Parfaits

INGREDIENTS

- ✓ 1 pint (2 cups) vanilla low-fat or vanilla frozen yogurt
- ✓ 2 cups fresh raspberries
- ✓ 1 1/2 cups Chocolate Cheerios cereal

INSTRUCTIONS

1) In 4 parfait glasses or clear drinking glasses, layer half of the frozen yogurt, half of the raspberries and half of the cereal. Repeat layers.

2) Serve immediately.

29. White Chocolate-Strawberry Yogurt Parfaits

INGREDIENTS

- ✓ 4 Nature Valley pecan crunch crunchy granola bars (2 pouches from 8.9-oz box), crushed (3/4 cup)
- ✓ 1/2 cup chopped pecans
- ✓ 1 package (3 oz) cream cheese, softened
- ✓ 1/2 cup whipped topping
- ✓ 1/2 cup marshmallow creme (from 7-oz jar)
- ✓ 1 oz white chocolate baking bar, shaved
- ✓ 1 container (6 oz) Fat Free white chocolate strawberry yogurt
- ✓ 1 cup sliced fresh strawberries
- ✓ Additional strawberry slices
- ✓ White chocolate curls
- ✓ Fresh mint leaves

INSTRUCTIONS

1) In small bowl, mix crushed granola bars and pecans; set aside. In large bowl, beat cream cheese with electric mixer on medium speed until smooth. Beat in whipped topping, marshmallow creme, shaved white chocolate and yogurt until well blended.

2) In each of 2 (14-oz) parfait glasses, layer 1/4 cup granola mixture, about 1/2 cup yogurt mixture and 1/4 cup sliced strawberries. Repeat layers. Top each parfait with 1 tablespoon remaining granola mixture. Garnish each with additional strawberry slices, white chocolate curls and mint leaves. Serve immediately.

30. Kiwi-Pineapple Yogurt Parfaits

INGREDIENTS

- 4 Nature Valley Oats 'n Honey crunchy granola bars (2 pouches from 8.9-oz box), unwrapped, broken into pieces
- 12 to 14 whole macadamia nuts
- 1 container (6 oz) Fat Free very vanilla yogurt
- 1/2 cup frozen (thawed) reduced-fat whipped topping
- 1 tablespoon shredded coconut
- 1 tablespoon finely grated white chocolate baking bar
- 1/2 cup coarsely chopped peeled kiwifruit (1 1/2 medium)
- 1/2 cup coarsely chopped drained fresh pineapple or well-drained canned pineapple tidbits
- 1 1/2 teaspoons honey
- White chocolate baking bar curls or shavings
- 2 kiwifruit slices

INSTRUCTIONS

1) In food processor or gallon-size resealable food-storage plastic bag, place granola bars and nuts; process or crush with meat mallet until chopped.
2) In small bowl, mix yogurt mixture ingredients until well blended; set aside. In another small bowl, gently toss fruit mixture ingredients until coated; set aside.
3) In each of 2 (12- to 14-oz) tulip-shaped parfait glasses, alternately spoon about 3 tablespoons granola mixture, 1/4 cup yogurt mixture and 1/4 cup fruit mixture; repeat layers. Top each parfait with a sprinkle of remaining granola mixture. Garnish each with white chocolate curls and kiwifruit slice. Serve immediately.

31. Crunchy Banana-Strawberry Parfaits

Here's a layered treat that combines sweet, smooth and crunchy in every bite!

INGREDIENTS

- ✓ 1 1/3 cups Fat Free creamy strawberry yogurt (from 2 lb container)
- ✓ 2 cups Cocoa Puff cereal
- ✓ 1/3 cup unsalted sunflower nuts
- ✓ 2 bananas, sliced
- ✓ 4 fresh whole strawberries

INSTRUCTIONS

1) For each serving, spoon 1/3 cup yogurt into dessert dish or parfait glass. Add 1/2 cup cereal. Top each with 1 tablespoon of the sunflower nuts, 1/4 of the banana slices and 1/4 of remaining yogurt.

2) Sprinkle with remaining sunflower nuts. Top each with strawberry.

32. Key Lime Parfaits

Add crunch to creamy parfaits for two with easy, buttery, homemade cereal squares.

INGREDIENTS

- ✓ 2 cups Cheerios cereal
- ✓ 3 tablespoons granulated sugar
- ✓ 2 tablespoons water
- ✓ 2 teaspoons butter, melted
- ✓ 1 cup frozen (thawed) fat-free whipped topping (4 oz)
- ✓ 1 tablespoon lime juice
- ✓ 2 containers (6 oz each) Fat Free Key lime pie yogurt

INSTRUCTIONS

1) Heat oven to 350°F. Spray cookie sheet and 12x12-inch sheet of foil with cooking spray. In food processor, place cereal and sugar; process with on-and-off motions until fine crumbs form. Add water and melted butter; process until thoroughly mixed.

2) Spread cereal mixture evenly in center of cookie sheet. Use foil, sprayed side down, to press cereal mixture slightly; roll with rolling pin into 12x8-inch rectangle, about 1/8 inch thick. With sharp knife, score mixture into 1-inch squares.

3) Bake 12 to 15 minutes or until squares are golden brown. Cool completely, about 10 minutes. Meanwhile, in small bowl, place whipped topping; fold in lime juice until blended.

4) Break cereal mixture apart at scored lines. Reserve 4 cereal squares; crumble remaining squares into small pieces. In each dessert bowl or 12-oz parfait glass, layer 1/4 cup crumbled cereal squares, half container of yogurt and scant 1/4 cup whipped topping mixture. Repeat layers. Top each parfait with 2 reserved cereal squares.

33. End-Of-The-Rainbow Cookie Parfaits

Kids and adults will flip for these easy rainbow parfaits that are easy to make and over-the-top delicious!

INGREDIENTS

- ✓ 1 roll (16.5 oz) Pillsbury refrigerated sugar cookies
- ✓ 2 eggs
- ✓ Red, orange, yellow, green and blue gel food colors
- ✓ 1 pint whipping cream
- ✓ 3 tablespoons sugar
- ✓ 1 teaspoon vanilla

INSTRUCTIONS

1) Heat oven to 350°F. Spray 10 regular-size muffin cups with cooking spray. Let cookie dough stand at room temperature 10 minutes to soften.

2) In large bowl, break up cookie dough; add eggs. Beat with electric mixer on medium speed until smooth and well combined. Divide dough evenly into 5 small bowls. Color dough with red, orange, yellow, green and blue food colors, stirring until well combined.

3) Scoop dough into muffin pans, making 2 cupcakes of each of the 5 colors, for a total of 10 cupcakes. Bake 15 to 18 minutes or until toothpick inserted in center comes out clean. Cool in pan 5 minutes. Remove cups from pan to cooling rack to cool completely, about 30 minutes.

4) Meanwhile, in medium bowl, beat whipping cream, sugar and vanilla with electric mixer on medium high speed until stiff peaks form.

5) Crumble each of the cupcakes, keeping the colors separate. Sprinkle red cake crumbles into each of 12 glass parfait cups, glasses or small jars. Pipe whipped cream on top of each. Repeat process with orange, yellow, green and blue cake crumbles, finishing with the blue cake crumbles. Serve immediately, or refrigerate until ready to serve.

34. Monster Cereal Pudding Parfaits

Everyone's three favorite monster cereals come together in one delicious no-bake layered Halloween dessert!

INGREDIENTS

- ✓ 1 (16 ounce) container whipped topping
- ✓ 1 packet chocolate pudding mix
- ✓ 1 (6 ounce) block cream cheese, softened
- ✓ 3 tablespoons sugar
- ✓ 1 cup Frankenberry cereal
- ✓ 1 cup Boo Berry cereal
- ✓ 1/2 cup Count Chocula cereal

INSTRUCTIONS

1) In a stand mixer, combine half of the whipped topping, pudding mix, cream cheese, and sugar. Beat until light and fluffy, about 2 minutes.
2) Spoon a small amount of the chocolate pudding mixture into the bottoms of 4 martini or parfait glasses. Top with a sprinkle of Frankenberry cereal.
3) Spoon a layer of the plain whipped topping next, followed by a sprinkle of Boo Berry cereal.

4) Add another layer of the chocolate pudding mixture (using the remainder), then top with a dollop of whipped topping and the remaining Frankenberry, Boo Berry, and Count Chocula cereals. Serve immediately.

35. Easy Pumpkin and Fudge Parfaits

INGREDIENTS

- 1 package Pillsbury Melts molten fudge cake filled cookies
- 1 cup whipped topping
- 2 containers (6 oz each) Light pumpkin pie yogurt
- Additional whipped topping

INSTRUCTIONS

1) Heat oven to 350°F.
2) Remove cookies from package; place about 2 inches apart on ungreased cookie sheet. Bake 11 to 15 minutes or until edges are set. Remove from cookie sheet to cooling rack; cool completely. (Reserve hot fudge packet for later use.)
3) Meanwhile, spoon 1 cup whipped topping and the yogurt into medium bowl. Using rubber spatula, gently fold together until well blended.
4) To assemble each of 4 parfaits, break 1 cookie into 4 pieces; place in bottom of tumbler or parfait glass. Spoon about 1/4 cup pumpkin mixture over cookie. Repeat with another layer of 1 broken cookie and 1/4 cup pumpkin mixture.
5) Top each parfait with small amount of additional whipped topping. Drizzle hot fudge from packet over top of parfaits.

36. Poison Apple Parfaits

Apple slices, yogurt, granola bars and a drizzle of caramel ... yum! Add a little edible disco dust to the apple top for an adorably "over the top" Snow White effect!

INGREDIENTS

- ✓ 4 medium sized apples
- ✓ 1 (6 oz container) Light Fat Free apple turnover yogurt
- ✓ 2 individual packs (2 bars each) Nature Valley Oats 'n Honey Crunchy Granola Bars
- ✓ 1/4 cup caramel sauce (any prepared caramel sauce or ice cream topping)
- ✓ 2 lemons
- ✓ 3 cups of water
- ✓ Edible cake decorating glitter or luster dust, if desired

INSTRUCTIONS

1) Cut tops off apples, and dust with the edible glitter or luster dust (if using) and set aside.
2) Slice each apple into 3 horizontal slices. Keep the slices from each individual apple grouped together for orderly parfaits.
3) Squeeze 2 lemons into about 3 cups of water, and dip the slices (not the glittery apple top though) into the lemon water to inhibit browning. Pat dry with paper towel.
4) Layer the yogurt, granola sauce between the apple slices.
5) Top each apple parfait with its glittery topper. Serve!

37. Plum Pudding Parfaits

INGREDIENTS

- 1 box (4-serving size) vanilla fat-free sugar-free instant pudding and pie filling mix
- 1 1/4 cups fat-free (skim) milk
- 1 cup Fat Free plain or Fat Free creamy vanilla yogurt (from 2-lb container)
- 1/2 cup low-fat granola
- 4 medium plums, pitted and chopped (about 2 cups)

INSTRUCTIONS

1) Make pudding mix as directed on box except use 1 1/4 cups fat-free (skim) milk. Fold in yogurt.

2) Place about 1/4 cup pudding mixture in bottom of each of 4 parfait glasses. Layer each with 1 tablespoon of the granola and about 1/4 cup of the plums; repeat layers. Top with remaining pudding mixture. Refrigerate until ready to serve.

38. Ambrosia Yogurt Parfaits

INGREDIENTS

- 3 containers (6 oz each) Fat Free French vanilla yogurt
- 1 can (8 oz) crushed pineapple in juice, drained
- 2 cups Honey Nut Cheerios cereal
- 1 medium banana, sliced (1 cup)
- 1 can (11 oz) mandarin orange segments in light syrup, drained
- 1/4 cup flaked coconut, toasted
- 4 fresh strawberries, sliced

INSTRUCTIONS

1) In medium bowl, mix yogurt and pineapple. Into each of 4 parfait glasses, place 1/4 cup of the cereal.

2) Spoon 2 tablespoons yogurt mixture on top of cereal in each glass. Top each with 1/4 cup cereal, then with 1/4 of the banana slices.

3) Spoon 2 tablespoons yogurt mixture onto banana in each; top each with orange segments. Spoon remaining yogurt mixture over orange segments. Sprinkle with coconut. Garnish with strawberries.

39. Berry Brownie Parfaits

INGREDIENTS

- 1 package (4-serving size) white chocolate instant pudding and pie filling mix
- 1 1/2 cups milk
- 1/2 teaspoon rum extract
- 1 cup frozen (thawed) whipped topping
- 4 brownies (2 1/2-inch square)
- 1 cup fresh raspberries

INSTRUCTIONS

1) Beat pudding mix, milk and rum extract in medium bowl 2 minutes, using wire whisk. Refrigerate 10 minutes. Fold in whipped topping.

2) Cut each brownie into 12 squares. For each serving, spoon about 2 tablespoons pudding mixture into 6- to 10-inch parfait glass. Top with 4 brownie pieces and 4 raspberries; press lightly. Repeat layers. Top each with 2 tablespoons pudding mixture. Refrigerate 30 minutes. Garnish with remaining raspberries.

40. Sun and Sky Yogurt Parfait

INGREDIENTS

- Orange gelatin
- Whipped topping
- Yoplait Key lime pie yogurt
- Fat Free Strawberry Mango Yogurt

INSTRUCTIONS

1) Prepare the gelatin per box instructions. Refrigerate until fully set.
2) Rake set gelatin with a fork to form globules.
3) Layer yogurt in parfait glasses, alternating with whipped topping to form clouds and sky. For the top layer add some orange gelatin for the sun.
4) Enjoy!!!

41. Cranberry Parfaits

INGREDIENTS

- ✓ 1 cup water
- ✓ 1 cup sugar
- ✓ 4 cups (1 12-oz. package) fresh cranberries, rinsed and picked over
- ✓ 6 cups Greek vanilla yogurt

INSTRUCTIONS

1) In a medium saucepan over high heat, stir together water and sugar and bring to a boil. Stir until sugar is dissolved.

2) Carefully add cranberries, taking care not to let the boiling water splatter. Return to a boil, then reduce heat to medium-low and simmer for about 10-15 minutes, until the cranberries begin to burst.

3) Remove from heat and let cool to room temperature. Then refrigerate until cool. (The cranberries will thicken as they cool.)

4) When cool, layer the cranberry sauce and Greek yogurt in small serving dishes to make mini-parfaits.

5) Optional: Top with a pinch of sugar or edible glitter for a sparkling touch!

42. Raspberry-Cookie Parfaits

INGREDIENTS

- ✓ 1 roll (16.5 oz) Pillsbury refrigerated chocolate chip cookies
- ✓ 1 box (4-serving size) chocolate instant pudding and pie filling mix
- ✓ 2 cups milk
- ✓ 1 container (8 oz) frozen whipped topping, thawed
- ✓ 1 can (21 oz) raspberry or cherry pie filling

INSTRUCTIONS

1) Heat oven to 350°F. Bake cookies as directed on package. Cool completely, about 15 minutes.
2) Meanwhile, make pudding as directed on box using milk; do not refrigerate.
3) Crumble enough cookies to make 2 1/2 cups; reserve remaining cookies for another use.
4) To assemble parfaits, in bottom of each of 10 (8-oz) parfait glasses or clear plastic drinking cups, layer about 1 tablespoon raspberry pie filling, 3 tablespoons cookie crumbs, 3 tablespoons pudding, about 1/4 cup whipped topping, 2 tablespoons pie filling and 1 tablespoon cookie crumbs. Top each with dollop of remaining whipped topping.

43. Raspberry Lemon Dessert Yogurt Parfaits

INGREDIENTS

- ✓ 10 fresh raspberries
- ✓ 1 container Fat Free raspberry yogurt
- ✓ 1 container Liberte Greek lemon yogurt or Liberte Mediterranee lemon yogurt
- ✓ 5 to 6 lemon shortbread cookies, crushed
- ✓ Grated lemon peel
- ✓ Additional crushed lemon shortbread cookie

INSTRUCTIONS

1) Set 2 raspberries aside for garnish. In medium bowl, mix and crush remaining raspberries. Stir in raspberry yogurt.

2) In 2 parfait glasses, spoon layer of raspberry mixture, using half of the mixture. Top each with lemon yogurt, using the entire lemon yogurt. Sprinkle layer of crushed cookies over lemon yogurt. Top with remaining raspberry yogurt.

3) Garnish with reserved raspberries, lemon peel and the additional crushed cookie. Refrigerate until ready to serve.

44. Chocolate Crunch Cheesecake Parfait

INGREDIENTS

- ✓ 1 package (8 oz) cream cheese, softened
- ✓ 1 container (8 oz) frozen whipped topping (thawed)
- ✓ 1/2 cup sour cream
- ✓ 1/4 cup powdered sugar
- ✓ 1/2 teaspoon vanilla
- ✓ 1/2 cup blackberry jam
- ✓ 3 cups fresh blackberries
- ✓ 1 1/2 cups Nature Valley oats 'n dark chocolate protein granola

INSTRUCTIONS

1) In medium bowl, beat Cheesecake ingredients with electric mixer on medium speed until smooth.
2) In medium microwavable bowl, microwave blackberry jam uncovered on High 30 seconds or until melted. Stir in blackberries.
3) In 6 parfait glasses, layer cheesecake mixture, berry filling and granola. Serve immediately, or refrigerate up to 1 hour before serving.

45. Chocolate-Kiwi-Berry Parfaits

INGREDIENTS

- ✓ 2 brownies (2x2-inches each), broken into pieces
- ✓ 12 medium strawberries, cut into chunks
- ✓ 2 medium kiwifruit, peeled, cut into chunks
- ✓ 2 cups Fat Free creamy strawberry or creamy vanilla yogurt (from 2-lb container)

INSTRUCTIONS

1) Reserve 1 tablespoon small brownie pieces for garnish. In each of 4 serving glasses, layer the remaining brownie pieces, the strawberries and kiwifruit.

2) Top each with 1/2 cup yogurt. Garnish each parfait with reserved brownie pieces. Serve immediately.

46. Fudgy-Peanut Butter Banana Parfaits

INGREDIENTS

- ✓ 4 Pillsbury Ready to Bake! Big Deluxe Classics refrigerated peanut butter cup cookies (from 18-oz package)
- ✓ 1/4 cup whipped cream cheese (from 8-oz container)
- ✓ 3 tablespoons powdered sugar
- ✓ 2 tablespoons creamy peanut butter
- ✓ 1 container (6 oz) Yoplait Thick & Creamy banana yogurt
- ✓ 1/2 cup frozen (thawed) whipped topping
- ✓ 1 bar (2.1 oz) chocolate-covered crispy peanut-buttery candy, unwrapped, finely crushed
- ✓ 1/4 cup hot fudge topping

INSTRUCTIONS

1) Heat oven to 350°F. Place cookie dough rounds 2 inches apart on ungreased cookie sheet. Bake 14 to 18 minutes or until edges are golden brown. Cool 3 minutes; remove from cookie sheet. Cool completely, about 15 minutes.

2) Meanwhile, in medium bowl, beat cream cheese, powdered sugar, peanut butter and yogurt with electric mixer on low speed until blended. Fold in whipped topping and crushed candy with rubber spatula.

3) In small microwavable bowl, microwave fudge topping on High 25 to 30 seconds or until melted and drizzling consistency. Crumble 1 cookie into each of 2 (12- to 14-oz) parfait glasses. Top each with about 1/3 cup yogurt mixture; drizzle each with 1 tablespoon fudge topping. Repeat layers. Refrigerate at least 1 hour but no longer than 4 hours before serving.

47. Patriotic Parfaits

INGREDIENTS

- ✓ 8 oz fresh strawberries, chopped
- ✓ 1 container (8 oz) frozen whipped topping, thawed
- ✓ 6 oz fresh blueberries

INSTRUCTIONS

1) In each of 4 parfait glasses or wine glasses, layer strawberries, whipped topping and blueberries. Serve immediately or refrigerate until serving time.

48. Praline Peach Parfaits

INGREDIENTS

- ✓ 1 tablespoon butter or margarine
- ✓ 1 tablespoon sugar
- ✓ 1/2 cup chopped pecans
- ✓ 1 1/2 cups Cinnamon Burst Cheerios cereal
- ✓ 1 cup Fat Free harvest peach yogurt (from 2-lb container)
- ✓ 2 1/4 cups peeled cubed peaches (about 2 large)

INSTRUCTIONS

1) In 10-inch nonstick skillet, melt butter over low heat. Stir in sugar. Add pecans; cook 3 to 4 minutes, stirring frequently, until golden brown and sugar is dissolved. Remove from heat. Stir in cereal.

2) Into each of 4 parfait glasses, spoon 1/4 cup cereal mixture, 2 tablespoons yogurt, 1/3 cup peaches, 1/4 cup cereal mixture, 2 tablespoons yogurt and remaining cereal mixture. Top with remaining peaches. Serve immediately.

49. Fresh Strawberry and Rhubarb Sauce Parfaits

INGREDIENTS

- ✓ 2 cups chopped fresh rhubarb
- ✓ 1 cup granulated sugar
- ✓ 1/4 cup cranberry-apple drink
- ✓ 3 cups sliced fresh strawberries
- ✓ 1 cup whipping cream
- ✓ 1 tablespoon powdered sugar
- ✓ 1 teaspoon vanilla
- ✓ 1 package (16 oz) frozen pound cake loaf, thawed, cubed

INSTRUCTIONS

1) In 2-quart saucepan, cook rhubarb, granulated sugar and drink over medium heat 10 to 15 minutes, stirring occasionally, until rhubarb is tender and mixture is syrupy.

2) Add 1 cup of the strawberries; cook and stir 1 to 2 minutes, mashing slightly. Remove from heat. Stir in remaining strawberries. Cool slightly. Refrigerate at least 1 hour until chilled.

3) Just before serving, in medium bowl, beat whipping cream, powdered sugar and vanilla until stiff peaks form. In each of 8 parfait glasses, layer sauce, cake cubes and whipped cream; repeat layers. Serve immediately. If desired, garnish each serving with fresh strawberry slice.

50. Frosted Toast Crunch Berry Parfaits

INGREDIENTS

- ✓ 2 cups Greek 100 plain yogurt (from 32-oz container)
- ✓ 1 tablespoon honey
- ✓ 1 teaspoon ground cinnamon
- ✓ 1/2 cup fresh blackberries
- ✓ 1/2 cup fresh blueberries
- ✓ 1 cup Frosted Toast Crunch cereal

INSTRUCTIONS

1) In small bowl, mix yogurt, honey and cinnamon. In another small bowl, mix berries.

2) In each of 4 small glasses or bowls, place 2 tablespoons of the cereal. Top cereal in each with 1/4 cup of the yogurt mixture and 2 tablespoons of the berry mixture. Repeat layers. Serve immediately.

51. Trix Very Berry Parfaits

INGREDIENTS

- ✓ 1 cup Trix cereal
- ✓ 1/2 cup fresh blueberries
- ✓ 1 container (6 oz) Fat Free mixed berry yogurt

INSTRUCTIONS

1) Place cereal in food-storage plastic bag; seal bag and slightly crush rolling pin or soup can.

2) In each of 2 (8-oz) parfait or drinking glasses, layer half of the berries and half of the yogurt. Top each parfait with half of the crushed cereal. Serve immediately.

52. Pumpkin Parfaits

INGREDIENTS

- 1 3/4 cups cold milk
- 1 box (4-serving size) vanilla instant pudding and pie filling mix
- 1 cup canned pumpkin (not pumpkin pie mix)
- 1/2 teaspoon pumpkin pie spice
- 1 package (8 oz) cream cheese, softened
- 3/4 cup powdered sugar
- 1 1/2 cups whipping cream
- 6 amaretti cookies

INSTRUCTIONS

1) In medium bowl, stir milk and pudding mix with whisk 2 minutes. Stir in pumpkin and pumpkin pie spice. Refrigerate until ready to assemble parfaits.

2) In another medium bowl, beat cream cheese and powdered sugar with electric mixer on low speed until blended and smooth. In chilled large bowl, beat whipping cream on high speed until stiff peaks form. Fold whipped cream into cream cheese mixture.

3) In each of 6 parfait glasses, spoon 1/4 cup pumpkin pudding; top each with 6 tablespoons cream cheese mousse mixture. Repeat layers. Refrigerate 2 hours or until serving time. Just before serving, top each parfait with a cookie.

53. Coconut Pumpkin Parfaits

INGREDIENTS

- 2 tablespoons butter or margarine
- 1/4 cup packed brown sugar
- 1 tablespoon water
- 1/4 cup chopped almonds (2 oz)
- 1/4 cup chopped pecans (2 oz)
- 4 oz cream cheese (from 8-oz package), softened
- 1/2 cup canned pumpkin (not pumpkin pie mix)
- 1/4 cup granulated sugar
- 1/2 teaspoon vanilla
- 1/4 teaspoon pumpkin pie spice
- 1/2 cup whipped cream (1/4 cup before whipping)
- 2 containers (6 oz each) Liberté Méditerranée coconut yogurt

INSTRUCTIONS

1) In 10-inch skillet, melt butter over medium heat. Stir in remaining nut topping ingredients; cook 1 to 2 minutes, stirring occasionally, until sugar is dissolved and nuts are golden brown. Set aside.
2) In medium bowl, beat cream cheese, pumpkin, granulated sugar, vanilla and pumpkin pie spice with electric mixer on medium speed until smooth and creamy. Gently fold in whipped cream.
3) Into each of 8 (2- to 3-oz) glasses, layer 2 tablespoons mousse, 2 tablespoons yogurt, 2 tablespoons mousse and 2 tablespoons nut topping.

54. Blueberry Trifle Parfaits

INGREDIENTS

- 1 (3.3-oz.) pkg. instant white chocolate flavor pudding and pie filling mix
- 1 1/2 cups milk
- 1/4 cup sugar
- 2 teaspoons cornstarch
- Dash nutmeg
- 1/4 cup water
- 1 pint (2 cups) fresh blueberries
- 4 (3/4-inch-thick) slices frozen pound cake, thawed, cut into 3/4-inch cubes
- 1/4 cup frozen whipped topping, thawed

INSTRUCTIONS

1) Prepare pudding as directed on package using the 1 1/2 cups milk. Refrigerate while preparing blueberry mixture.
2) Meanwhile, in medium saucepan, combine sugar, cornstarch and nutmeg; mix well. Add water and 1 cup of the blueberries; mix well. Bring to a boil. Reduce heat to medium-low; simmer 5 minutes or until slightly thickened, stirring occasionally. Refrigerate 10 minutes or until slightly cooled.
3) Stir in remaining 1 cup blueberries. Refrigerate at least 30 minutes or until cold.
4) In 4 parfait glasses or dessert dishes, layer half each of cake cubes, pudding and blueberry mixture. Repeat layers. Top with whipped topping. Store in refrigerator.

55. Homemade Eggnog Ice Cream Parfaits

INGREDIENTS

- 1 jar (10 oz) maraschino cherries, drained
- 1 pint (2 cups) whipping cream, chilled
- 1 can (14 oz) sweetened condensed milk (not evaporated)
- 1/2 teaspoon ground cinnamon
- 1/4 teaspoon ground nutmeg
- 1 tablespoon rum extract
- 2 teaspoons vanilla
- 12 jelly jars or drinking glasses (8 oz each)
- 3 cups Cinnamon Toast Crunch cereal

INSTRUCTIONS

1) Reserve 12 whole cherries for garnish. Chop remaining cherries; set aside.
2) In medium bowl, beat whipping cream with electric mixer on high speed until stiff peaks form.
3) In large bowl, stir together condensed milk, cinnamon, nutmeg, rum extract and vanilla. Fold in whipped cream until combined.
4) To make each parfait in jelly jar or glass, layer about 1 tablespoon cereal, about 1/4 cup cream mixture, some of the chopped cherries, another tablespoon cereal and a layer of cream mixture. Sprinkle top with cereal; top with 1 reserved whole cherry.
5) Cover; freeze at least 5 to 6 hours before serving.

56. Healthified Tiramisu Parfaits

INGREDIENTS

- 4 oz (half of 8-oz package) 1/3-less-fat cream cheese (Neufchâtel), softened
- 3/4 cup reduced-fat ricotta cheese
- 1/2 cup powdered sugar
- 1 teaspoon vanilla
- 1 container (6 oz) Fat Free French vanilla yogurt
- 1/3 cup cold brewed espresso or strong coffee
- 2 tablespoons coffee-flavored liqueur, cold brewed espresso or strong coffee
- 1 package (3 oz) soft ladyfingers, cut into 1/2-inch cubes
- 1 oz semisweet baking chocolate, grated (1/4 cup)

INSTRUCTIONS

1) In medium bowl, beat cream cheese with electric mixer on medium speed until smooth. Beat in ricotta cheese, powdered sugar and vanilla until creamy. Beat in yogurt until well blended. In small bowl, mix espresso and liqueur.

2) In 8 small parfait glasses or clear drinking glasses, layer half of the ladyfingers, half of the espresso mixture and half of the cheese mixture. Sprinkle each with about 3/4 teaspoon grated chocolate. Repeat layers.

3) Cover; refrigerate at least 1 hour to blend flavors but no longer than 4 hours. Store covered in refrigerator.

57. Creamy Caramel-Peach Parfaits

INGREDIENTS

- 2/3 cup caramel topping
- 1 container (8 ounces) frozen whipped topping, thawed
- 5 soft molasses cookies, broken up
- 1 can (29 ounces) sliced peaches, drained and cut into pieces
- Additional soft molasses cookies, crumbled, if desired

INSTRUCTIONS

1) Fold caramel topping into whipped topping in small bowl.

2) Layer broken cookies, topping mixture and peaches in 6 parfait or other tall glasses. Sprinkle with cookie crumbs. Serve immediately, or refrigerate until serving.

58. Vanilla Cupcakes, Blueberry And Whipped Topping Jar Parfaits

INGREDIENTS

- ✓ 1 box Betty Crocker SuperMoist natural vanilla or French vanilla cake mix
- ✓ Water, vegetable oil and eggs called for on cake mix box
- ✓ 1 package (8 oz) cream cheese, softened
- ✓ 1 container (8 oz) frozen whipped topping, thawed
- ✓ 1 can (21 oz) blueberry pie filling
- ✓ 24 (8-oz) jelly jars with lids

INSTRUCTIONS

1) Heat oven to 350°F. Place paper baking cup in each of 24 regular-size muffin cups. Make and bake cake mix as directed on box for 24 cupcakes. Cool in pans 10 minutes; remove from pans to cooling rack. Cool completely, about 30 minutes.

2) In large bowl, beat cream cheese and whipped topping with electric mixer on low speed just until combined, about 1 minute, then on high speed about 2 minutes or until creamy.

3) Cut each cupcake horizontally in half. For each parfait, place bottom half of cupcake in jar. Spoon 1 tablespoon whipped topping mixture over cupcake, then 1 tablespoon pie filling over whipped topping mixture; repeat layering, beginning with top half of cupcake. Cover jars with lids and refrigerate until ready to serve.

59. Neapolitan Shortcake Parfaits

INGREDIENTS

- 4 cups sliced fresh strawberries
- 1/2 cup granulated sugar
- 2 1/4 cups Gold Medal all-purpose flour
- 3 tablespoons granulated sugar
- 2 1/2 teaspoons baking powder
- 1 teaspoon salt
- 3/4 cup milk
- 1/2 cup butter or margarine, melted
- 1 bag (6 oz) semisweet chocolate chips (1 cup)
- 1 tablespoon shortening
- 1 1/2 cups whipping cream
- 1/3 cup powdered sugar
- 1 teaspoon vanilla
- Additional strawberries, if desired

INSTRUCTIONS

1) Heat oven to 425°F. Lightly grease cookie sheet with shortening. In medium bowl, mix strawberries and 1/2 cup granulated sugar; set aside.

2) To make shortcakes, in medium bowl, mix flour, 3 tablespoons granulated sugar, the baking powder and salt. Stir in milk and butter until soft dough forms. Onto cookie sheet, drop dough by 8 heaping tablespoonfuls. Bake 10 to 12 minutes or until golden brown. Remove from cookie sheet to cooling rack. Cool completely.

3) In small microwavable bowl, microwave chocolate chips and shortening uncovered on Medium 1 to 2 minutes, stirring after 1 minute, until melted.

4) In chilled medium bowl, beat whipping cream, powdered sugar and vanilla with electric mixer on high speed until soft peaks form.

5) Break shortcakes into bite-size pieces. In parfait glasses, alternate layers of shortcake, strawberries, chocolate mixture and whipped cream. Garnish with additional strawberries.

60. Chocolate-Banana Pudding Parfaits

INGREDIENTS

- ✓ 1 box (6-serving size) chocolate instant pudding and pie filling mix
- ✓ 2 1/2 cups milk
- ✓ 1 can (14 oz) sweetened condensed milk (not evaporated)
- ✓ 1 container (8 oz) frozen whipped topping, thawed
- ✓ 1 package (9 oz) thin chocolate wafer cookies
- ✓ 4 ripe large bananas, sliced
- ✓ 1 square (1 oz) semisweet chocolate, shaved

INSTRUCTIONS

1) In large bowl, beat pudding mix and milk with wire whisk about 2 minutes or until well blended. Let stand 5 minutes or until thickened. Stir in condensed milk. Fold in 1 1/2 cups of the whipped topping.

2) Reserve 15 cookies for garnish; crush remaining cookies. Divide crushed cookies evenly among 15 lowball glasses or glass dessert dishes. Layer evenly with 3 of the sliced bananas and the pudding mixture. Just before serving, top each parfait with remaining whipped topping. Garnish with remaining sliced banana, reserved whole cookies and the chocolate shavings.

61. Tiramisu With Cookie Crisp

No need to hunt around the store and cross your fingers that you'll find yourself a batch of ladyfingers! This delicious tiramisu parfait calls for Cookie Crisp. So good, it's downright naughty!

INGREDIENTS

- ✓ 2 cups heavy whipping cream
- ✓ 1/2 cup instant toffee-flavored coffee powdered drink mix
- ✓ 1/2 cup rum
- ✓ 8 ounces cream cheese or mascarpone cheese, softened
- ✓ 1/2 cup sugar
- ✓ 2 cups Cookie Crisp Cereal
- ✓ 1/4 cup grated dark chocolate
- ✓ Raspberries or cranberries & mint leaves for garnish

INSTRUCTIONS

1) In an electric mixer, beat together the cream, coffee powder, rum, cream cheese, and sugar, until light and fluffy.
2) Spoon a small amount of the cream mixture into the bottom of four wine glasses.
3) Top with a layer of Cookie Crisp, then another layer of the cream mixture.
4) Sprinkle grated chocolate on top of each wine glass.
5) Cover tightly with plastic wrap and allow the desserts to sit in the fridge overnight. Though you can serve them right away, preparing them the day before allows the Cookie Crisp, to soften to a cake-like consistency, just like ladyfingers!
6) Garnish if desired. Serve and enjoy.

62. Peanut Butter Cheerios Pudding Carnival

INGREDIENTS

- ✓ 1/2 firm ripe banana, sliced
- ✓ 1 container (3.6 oz) refrigerated sugar-free vanilla pudding (60 calories or less)
- ✓ 1/2 cup Multi Grain Cheerios peanut butter cereal
- ✓ 1 teaspoon fat-free or low-fat caramel dip
- ✓ 2 teaspoons chopped dry-roasted peanuts

INSTRUCTIONS

1) Place banana slices in medium bowl or parfait glass. Top with pudding; add cereal.
2) Drizzle with caramel; sprinkle with peanuts.

63. Luscious Lemon Bar Parfait

INGREDIENTS

- ✓ 1 Fiber One 90 calorie lemon bar
- ✓ 1/2 cup reduced-fat whipped topping, thawed
- ✓ 3/4 teaspoon grated lemon peel
- ✓ 1/2 teaspoon fresh lemon juice

INSTRUCTIONS

1) Cut lemon bar into 12 bite-size pieces. In small bowl, mix whipped topping, 1/2 teaspoon of the lemon peel and the lemon juice. In small serving glass, layer half of lemon bar pieces and half of whipped topping mixture. Repeat layers with remaining lemon bar pieces and whipped topping mixture. Garnish with remaining 1/4 teaspoon lemon peel. Serve immediately.

64. Apple Cinnamon Parfait

INGREDIENTS

- 1 Fiber One 90 calorie cinnamon coffee cake (from 5.34-oz box)
- 1/4 cup Yoplait Light apple turnover yogurt (from 6-oz container)
- 1/4 cup diced Granny Smith apple

INSTRUCTIONS

1) Cut cinnamon coffee cake into 12 bite-size pieces. In small serving glass, layer half of cake pieces and half of the yogurt. Repeat layers; top with diced apple. Serve immediately.

65. Butterscotch Mousse Parfait

INGREDIENTS

- 1 Fiber One 90 calorie chocolate peanut butter brownie
- 2 tablespoons whipped topping
- 1/2 fat-free, sugar-free butterscotch pudding
- 3 pretzel sticks

INSTRUCTIONS

1) Cut a chocolate peanut butter brownie into bite-sized pieces. Then, place half the brownie bites into the bottom of a bowl, layering on butterscotch pudding and whipped topping. Repeat with another layer of each. Add pretzels and enjoy.

66. St. Patrick's Day Parfait

INGREDIENTS

- 1 Fiber One 90 calorie mint fudge brownie, crumbled
- 3 tbsp. prepared fat-free white chocolate pudding
- 1/2 tsp. crème de menthe liqueur (green)
- 1/4 tsp. green coarse sugar

INSTRUCTIONS

1) In a small bowl, stir pudding and crème de menthe. Dip the edge of a small mug in pudding and sugar, then layer pudding and crumbled brownie. Sprinkle green sugar on top and dig into this adult parfait.

67. Key Lime Pie Parfait

INGREDIENTS

- ✓ 2 graham crackers, crushed (about 1/3 cup)
- ✓ 1 tablespoon butter, melted
- ✓ 1 container (5.3 oz) Yoplait Greek 2% Key lime pie yogurt
- ✓ 1 lime slice

INSTRUCTIONS

1) In small bowl, stir together crushed crackers and butter. Set aside 1 teaspoon of crumb mixture.

2) Spoon half of the remaining crumb mixture in bottom of parfait cup. Top with half of the yogurt. Repeat layers, and garnish with reserved crumb mixture and lime slice.

68. Red Velvet Parfaits

INGREDIENTS

- ✓ 4 containers (6 oz each) Yoplait Light Fat Free red velvet yogurt
- ✓ 4 containers (6 oz each) Yoplait Light Fat Free very vanilla yogurt
- ✓ 4 teaspoons seedless raspberry jam
- ✓ 1 package (0.81 oz) chocolate thin crisp cookies, crushed

INSTRUCTIONS

1) In each of 4 tall parfait glasses, place 1/2 container red velvet yogurt; top with 1/2 container vanilla yogurt. Spoon 1 teaspoon jam over vanilla yogurt in each. Repeat with remaining yogurts. Top each with 1 tablespoon crushed cookies.

2) Serve immediately, or refrigerate before serving.

69. Black-Bottom Strawberry Cream Parfaits

INGREDIENTS

- ✓ 1 package (8 oz) 1/3-less-fat cream cheese (Neufchâtel), softened
- ✓ 1/2 cup powdered sugar
- ✓ 1 tablespoon grated orange peel
- ✓ 1 cup frozen (thawed) whipped topping
- ✓ 16 thin chocolate wafer cookies, finely crushed
- ✓ 16 fresh whole strawberries, cut into 1/4-inch-thick slices
- ✓ 8 teaspoons chocolate topping

INSTRUCTIONS

1) In small bowl, beat cream cheese, powdered sugar and orange peel until smooth. Gently stir in whipped topping.

2) Just before serving, into each of 8 parfait glasses, layer 2 tablespoons cookie crumbs, 2 tablespoons cream cheese mixture, several strawberry slices and 1 teaspoon chocolate topping.

70. Crunchy-Topped Strawberry-Kiwi Parfaits

INGREDIENTS

- ✓ 2 cups Banana Nut Cheerios cereal
- ✓ 1/4 cup sliced almonds
- ✓ 1 1/2 cups Fat Free creamy vanilla or creamy harvest peach yogurt (from 2-lb container)
- ✓ 1 cup sliced fresh strawberries
- ✓ 2 medium kiwifruit, peeled, cut into chunks

INSTRUCTIONS

1) Heat oven to 350°F. Place cereal and almonds in ungreased 13x9-inch pan. Bake 6 to 10 minutes, stirring occasionally, until light brown. Cool about 5 minutes.

2) In each of 4 parfait glasses, alternate layers of yogurt, strawberries, kiwifruit and toasted cereal and almond mixture. Serve immediately.

71. Mango Parfait

INGREDIENTS

- ✓ 2 large, ripe mangos, pitted and cubed
- ✓ 3 c low fat vanilla yogurt
- ✓ 6 Tbsp low fat granola

INSTRUCTIONS

1) Puree 1 mango and spoon equal amounts into 6 clear plastic cups.

2) Top each with 1/4 cup yogurt.

3) Spoon cubed mango over the top, saving a few pieces for garnish.

4) Top with remaining 1/4 cup yogurt and reserved mango.

5) (Recipe may be made ahead at this point. Cover and refrigerate until ready to serve.)

72. Vanilla & Mocha Parfaits Mini's

INGREDIENTS

- 6 slice poundcake
- 1 pkg vanilla pudding
- 1/3 c kahlua or coffee liquor
- 2 c cool whip, defrosted
- 3 Tbsp chocolate syrup
- 2 Tbsp slivered almonds toasted lightly
- 1/2 Tbsp mini milk chocolate chips
- 1- 1 1/2 Tbsp confectioners' sugar
- 2 tsp cocoa powder
- 2 tsp espresso powder, instant

INSTRUCTIONS

1) Slice off the required amounts of poundcake and cube small, place on a plate and set aside. In a small bowl, prepare your vanilla pudding using the instructions on the package. Set aside. Using a small saute pan, place on stove at medium high heat. Add your slivered almonds and toast for about 1-2 minutes till edges are lightly starting to toast. Turn off heat and set aside.

2) Layering: Add your cubed cake cubes to the bottom of your parfait glasses. Drizzle with Kahlua, and a drizzle of chocolate syrup. Next add your vanilla pudding to almost to the top of each parfait glass. Set aside.

3) In a bowl add your defrosted cool whip, sprinkle in the confectioner's sugar, the cocoa and the espresso powder. Mix till all thoroughly incorporated. Place in a pastry bag (if desired), or just spoon topping ontop of parfaits. Place a mini chocolate chip in

center of each parfaits. Decorate sides with slivered almonds standing on end. When you serve this, whatch the smile of your guests, that is the best thank you, a cook can ever have!!!

73. Cherry and Amaretti Parfaits

INGREDIENTS

- ✓ 6 ounces (1 cup) dried cherries
- ✓ 1 cup water
- ✓ 1/2 cup granulated sugar
- ✓ 1/4 teaspoon coarse salt
- ✓ 6 ounces cream cheese, softened
- ✓ 3/4 cup part-skim ricotta
- ✓ 1/2 teaspoon pure vanilla extract
- ✓ 1/4 cup confectioners' sugar
- ✓ 8 amaretti cookies, coarsely crumbled

INSTRUCTIONS

1) Combine cherries, water, granulated sugar, and 1/8 teaspoon salt in a small saucepan over medium heat. Bring to a simmer, and cook, stirring occasionally, for 20 minutes. Let cool.
2) Meanwhile, blend cream cheese, ricotta, vanilla, confectioners' sugar, and remaining 1/8 teaspoon salt in a food processor until smooth. Divide cherries among 4 glasses, then top each with ricotta mixture. Sprinkle tops with crumbled amaretti cookies, and serve immediately.

74. Gingersnap and Jam Parfaits

INGREDIENTS

- 3/4 cup red-currant jam or jelly
- 3 tablespoons fresh lemon juice
- 1/2 cup creme fraiche or sour cream
- 3/4 cup heavy cream
- 1/4 cup sugar
- 3/4 teaspoon pure vanilla extract
- 1/4 teaspoon ground cardamom
- 1/4 teaspoon ground ginger
- 8 (about 1/2 cup) gingersnap, cookies crushed

INSTRUCTIONS

1) Whisk together jam and lemon juice in a small bowl; set aside. Beat the creme fraiche, cream, sugar, vanilla, and spices with an electric mixer until mixture holds stiff peaks. Gently fold in 1 tablespoon jam mixture with a rubber spatula, creating red swirls.

2) Layer 1 heaping tablespoon cream mixture, 1 tablespoon crushed cookies, and 1 tablespoon jam mixture in a small glass. Repeat layering; top with a dollop of cream mixture. Make 3 more parfaits. Refrigerate until ready to serve, up to 1 hour.

75. Emeril's Late-Night Parfaits

INGREDIENTS

- ✓ 1 pint vanilla ice cream
- ✓ 1/2 cup crumbled biscotti cookies or other cookie crumbs of choice
- ✓ 1/4 cup Frangelico or other nut-flavored liqueur
- ✓ 2 tablespoons roughly chopped hazelnuts or walnuts, lightly toasted

INSTRUCTIONS

1) Remove the ice cream from the freezer and let it soften slightly, about 5 minutes at room temperature.

2) Into the bottom of four parfait or ice cream dishes, scoop about 2 tablespoons of the vanilla ice cream. Top with about 1/2 tablespoon of the cookie crumbs, and drizzle with 1 1/2 teaspoons of the liqueur. Continue layering the ingredients, ending with liqueur on top.

3) Serve immediately, garnished with the chopped nuts.

76. Savory Tomato Parfaits

INGREDIENTS

- 8 oz medium dark heirloom tomatoes, such as Black Krim cored and chopped
- salt
- 8 oz yellow plum tomatoes, cored and chopped
- 1 tsp chopped parsley
- 1/4 tsp thyme leaf
- a few drops of white wine vinegar
- 8 oz red cherry tomatoes, halved
- breadsticks, for garnish

INSTRUCTIONS

1) In a blender, puree the dark tomatoes at high speed, until very smooth, 2 minutes; scrape down the sides as necessary. Season the puree with salt and carefully pour into 4 glasses. Refrigerate for about 30 minutes, until the puree has firmed up slightly.

2) Rinse and dry the blender. Repeat the pureeing process with the yellow tomatoes. Add the parsley, thyme and vinegar; season with salt. Carefully pour the yellow puree into the glasses and refrigerate for about 15 minutes, until the yellow puree is set.

3) Rinse and dry the blender and process the cherry tomatoes to make the top layer of the parfaits. Refrigerate for 30 minutes. Garnish with breadsticks and serve.

77. Mango & Raspberry Parfait

INGREDIENTS

- 3 ripe organic mangos
- 1/2 cup of raspberries
- 1/4 cup of goji berries
- 2 tablespoons of raw honey
- 1 teaspoon of ground cardamom
- 1 cup of raw walnuts
- 1/4 cup of unsweetened shredded coconut

INSTRUCTIONS

1) To make the mango purée (also the base for the raspberry and goji berry whip):
2) 1. Cut each mango in half, just clearing the long flat seed.
3) 2. Peel the mango halves and puree in a high speed blender.
4) 3. Remove half the mango puree from the blender and keep in a container in the fridge. With the remaining mango purée, proceed to making the raspberry and goji berry whip.

5) Making the raspberry and goji berry whip is super easy. Add half the raspberries (1/4 cup) plus the goji berries into a Vitamix (or high speed blender) with the remainder of the mango purée. Process until it is smooth to perfection. If you don't have a Vitamix (or a powerful blender), you might want to soak the goji berries overnight instead of using them dry. Make sure to drain them before combining with the raspberries so they do not alter the consistent of the whip by making it too runny. Put in a container (separate from the mango purée) and refrigerate while you move on to the walnut/cardamom crumble.

6) To make the Walnut/Cardamom crumble: Place the walnuts, shredded coconut, cardamom, and raw honey in a food processor using the S-shaped blade and pulse until you achieve a nice crumbly texture. Make sure you don't overdo it. You don't want the crumble to get too fine and sticky.

7) I adore cardamom. To me it's the scent of India (with tuberose and nag champa of course). This is where I was first introduced to cardamom. It's used in so many Indian sweets and recipes that it instantly brings back wonderful memories. Plus, cardamom and coconut are a match made in heaven. There's a traditional Indian sweet called burfi I used to go crazy for (before my raw vegan days). It's funny because I don't really have a sweet tooth, but this dessert cast a spell on me to the point where my adoptive Indian "dad" had to ration it!

8) Okay, you've got the mango purée, the raspberry and goji berry whip, and the walnut/cardamom crumble ready. Now is time to assemble. That's my favorite part…! Scoop a couple spoonfuls of mango purée into a parfait glass. Follow with a layer of crumble, and finish off with a couple spoonfuls of berry whip. Sprinkle some crumble on top and use the remaining raspberries as decoration for a punch of vibrant color.

9) Look at these glorious raspberries. They're color therapy to me!

10) Now all you have to do is enjoy a healthy treat and a very Merry Christmas!

78. Banana Chai Smoothie Parfait

INGREDIENTS

- 5 frozen bananas
- 1 cup chai tea ice cubes (directions in notes)
- 2 tbsp coconut cream or coconut yogurt
- 1 tbsp almond butter
- 6 pitted dates
- ½ tsp pure vanilla extract
- 1 pinch cinnamon
- 1 pinch dried ginger
- granola
- coconut yogurt
- fresh blueberries
- chopped apricots
- maple syrup (Pure Infused's Lavender Chai is a great way to enhance the chai flavour!)

INSTRUCTIONS

1) In a high speed blender combine all ingredients (minus toppings) and blend on high until creamy and smooth.
2) If the consistency isn't thick enough, place in a bowl and freeze for 30 minutes to 1 hour, stirring often.
3) Scoop half of the banana chai smoothie into a bowl or glass. Top with ½ cup of granola, fresh blueberries, chopped apricots, a dollop of coconut yogurt and a drizzle of maple syrup. Enjoy!

79. Strawberry Frozen Yogurt Parfaits

INGREDIENTS

- ✓ 1 pint Yoplait Original Frozen Yogurt Strawberry
- ✓ 2 cups sliced strawberries
- ✓ 1 graham cracker

INSTRUCTIONS

1) Let the frozen yogurt sit out until slightly softened.

2) Put a layer of strawberries on the bottom of 4 parfait glasses. Add about ¼ cup of Yoplait

3) Strawberry Original Frozen Yogurt on top of the strawberries and smooth as much as possible.

4) Add another layer of strawberries, then another ¼ cup of yogurt. Top with crumbled graham cracker. Serve immediately, or freeze until ready to serve.

80. Easy Breakfast Parfait

INGREDIENTS

- ✓ fresh blackberries (or other fruits/berries)
- ✓ bananas, peeled and sliced
- ✓ granola (or other favorite crunchy cereal)
- ✓ yogurt (I used honey-vanilla!)
- ✓ grated coconut
- ✓ nuts (almonds, walnuts, pecans, etc.)
- ✓ honey or agave nectar
- ✓ pinch of ground cinnamon

INSTRUCTIONS

1) In a small bowl or glass, layer the ingredients in whatever order you'd like. Serve immediately.

81. Twix Trifles

INGREDIENTS

- ✓ Twix bars (I used 3 packages), chopped into 1/4" pieces
- ✓ chocolate fudge sauce (homemade or storebought)
- ✓ whipped cream (homemade or storebought)
- ✓ salted caramel mousse (recipe below)
- ✓ 1/3 cup sugar
- ✓ 3 Tbsp. water
- ✓ 1/3 cup heavy cream
- ✓ 1 tsp. vanilla extract
- ✓ 1/4 tsp. sea salt (or more, to taste)
- ✓ 4 oz. PHILADELPHIA Cream Cheese
- ✓ 1 cup powdered sugar

INSTRUCTIONS

1) In a trifle bowl or small glass, add a layer of the chopped Twix bars. Then use a pastry bag (or a Ziplock bag with the corner tip

cut out) to pipe in a layer of caramel mouse. Then do the same with a layer of chocolate fudge sauce. Then repeat! Finish of with a layer of whipped cream, and top with the remaining Twix bars. Serve immediately or refrigerate up to 8 hours.

2) Briefly stir together granulated sugar and water in a small saucepan, then bring to a boil over medium-high heat. Continue cooking, without stirring, until mixture turns dark amber in color, about 6 to 7 minutes. (Keep an eye on it, though, because it goes from clear to amber very quickly!)

3) Remove from heat and slowly add in cream (just start with a tablespoon or two), stirring with a wooden spoon until completely smooth. (Be careful, as the mixture will definitely bubble up and possibly splatter a bit as you add in the cream.) Stir in vanilla and salt. Set aside until it reaches room temperature, or refrigerate to speed up the process.

4) In the bowl of a stand mixer, beat PHILADELPHIA Cream Cheese on medium-high speed for 1 minute until very smooth. Add in the room-temperature caramel and powdered sugar, and beat on medium-low speed until combined. If the mousse is too thick, add in a tablespoon or two of heavy cream. Then increase speed to medium-high and beat for another 2 minutes until light and fluffy. Set aside.

82. Roasted Cherry Parfait

INGREDIENTS

- 1 cup cherries, pitted
- 1 cup quick-cook oats
- ½ cup nuts (almonds, walnuts, pecans, or pistachios)
- 3 tablespoons shredded coconut
- 1 teaspoon honey
- 1 cup Greek yogurt

INSTRUCTIONS

1) Preheat oven to 400° F. Line a rimmed baking sheet with parchment paper or a silicon baking mat. Place cherries on one side of the baking sheet.

2) To make granola crumble, mix together oats, nuts, coconut and honey. Spread in an even layer on the other half of the baking sheet. Bake in the oven for 7-8 minutes. Remove and allow to cool slightly before assembling the parfait.

3) To assemble: spoon half of yogurt into the bottom of a small glass or serving dish. Top with half of granola crumble and then half of cherries. Repeat another layer of yogurt, then granola crumble and then cherries.

83. Roasted Peach Parfaits

INGREDIENTS

- 6 peaches, halved
- 2 tablespoons brown sugar
- 2 cups greek yogurt
- honey
- Pistachio Crumble Topping
- ¼ cup all-purpose flour
- ¼ cup brown sugar, packed
- 3 tablespoons butter
- ½ cup quick-cooking oats
- ½ cup chopped pistachios
- pinch salt

INSTRUCTIONS

1) Roasted Peaches. Preheat oven to 500° F.
2) Place peach halves onto a kitchen sheet pan with skin side down. Sprinkle each half of peach with brown sugar. Roast until peach halves have browned, about 3-5 minutes. Remove from oven and allow to cool slightly. Crumble Topping. Preheat oven to 350° F.
3) Cut butter into flour and brown sugar with a pastry blender or two forks in a medium bowl. Stir in oats, pistachios and salt. Spread onto a small kitchen sheet pan and toast, about 10 minutes. Remove from oven and allow to cool.
4) Place one roasted peach half in the bottom of a parfait dish or glass. Top with about ¼ cup greek yogurt. Drizzle with honey and sprinkle crumble topping on top. Serve immediately.

84. Vanilla Bean Yogurt and Nectarine Parfait With Candied Nuts

INGREDIENTS

- ✓ 4 (4 oz) Vanilla Bean Activia Dessert Cups
- ✓ 3 Nectarines (4 if smallish), diced large
- ✓ 1 wedge of Fresh Lemon (2 if you want it real lemony)
- ✓ 1 tablespoon White Granulated Sugar
- ✓ 4 oz Pecans
- ✓ 4 oz Walnuts
- ✓ 1/2 (scant) cup White Granulated Sugar
- ✓ 1/8 teaspoon Cinnamon
- ✓ 1/8 teaspoon Kosher Salt
- ✓ Egg Whites from one Egg

INSTRUCTIONS

1) Combine the Nectarines with the lemon juice and sugar. Toss, cover and refrigerate until ready to use.

2) Preheat oven to 250 degrees and butter a small baking sheet. Combine the sugar, cinnamon and salt in a small bowl and set aside. In a medium sized bowl whisk egg white with a splash of water until frothy. Add the nuts and toss until evenly coated. Next add the nuts to the cinnamon and sugar mixture and toss again until coated. Spread sugared nuts onto prepared baking sheet and bake for 30 minutes, tossing every 10 minutes. Let cool.

3) Add some of the nectarines to four glasses and top with a third of the vanilla bean yogurt. Layer with fruit again, then the other third of the yogurt and repeat one more time. Top with candied nuts and serve!

85. Cool & Creamy Oreo Parfaits

INGREDIENTS

- ✓ 1 regular size package Oreo Cookies, crushed into crumbs
- ✓ 3 cups whole milk
- ✓ 2 small boxes instant vanilla pudding
- ✓ 12 oz Cool Whip, thawed
- ✓ 1/4 cup (1/2 stick) salted butter, softened to room temperature
- ✓ 8 oz cream cheese, softened to room temperature
- ✓ 1 teaspoon vanilla extract
- ✓ 1 cup powdered sugar

INSTRUCTIONS

1) In a large bowl, whisk together milk and pudding mixes until thick. Refrigerate for about 30 minutes, until firm. Fold in Cool Whip and refrigerate while preparing the rest of the mixture.

2) IN the bowl of your mixer, beat butter, cream cheese and vanilla on medium speed until smooth. Slowly add powdered sugar and beat on medium speed for one minute, until smooth. Fold cream cheese mixture into pudding mixture with a rubber spatula until combined.

3) Spread cookie crumbs in bottom of dish. Layer pudding mix and cookie crumbs.

86. Grasshopper Parfaits

INGREDIENTS

- ✓ 36 cool mint oreo cookies, finely chopped
- ✓ 3 cups whole milk
- ✓ 2 packages instant vanilla pudding
- ✓ 12 ounces cool whip, thawed
- ✓ 1/4 cup salted butter, softened to room temperature
- ✓ 8 ounces cream cheese, softened to room temperature
- ✓ 1/4 teaspoon pure vanilla extract
- ✓ 1 1/4 teaspoons mint extract
- ✓ 1 cup powdered sugar
- ✓ 2-3 drops green food coloring

INSTRUCTIONS

1) In a large bowl, whisk together milk and pudding mixes until thick. Refrigerate for about 30 minutes, until firm. Fold in Cool Whip and refrigerate while preparing the rest of the mixture.
2) In the bowl of your mixer, beat butter, cream cheese and extracts on medium speed until smooth.
3) Slowly add powdered sugar and beat on medium speed for one minute, until smooth.
4) Fold cream cheese mixture into pudding mixture with a rubber spatula until combined.
5) Fold in green food coloring until combined.
6) Spread cookie crumbs in bottom of dish.
7) Layer pudding mix and cookie crumbs.

87. Carrot Cake Parfaits

INGREDIENTS

- ✓ 12 1/2 pint canning jars
- ✓ Carrot Cake, baked and cooled (I used Duncan Hines Decadent Carrot Cake Mix, baked in two 9 inch round pans)
- ✓ Mousse:
- ✓ 8 oz block cream cheese, softened
- ✓ 1/3 cup orange juice
- ✓ 1/2 cup powdered sugar
- ✓ 8 oz tub Cool Whip
- ✓ Frosting:
- ✓ 8 oz block cream cheese, softened
- ✓ 1 stick (1/2 cup) butter, softened
- ✓ 1 teaspoon vanilla

- ✓ 4 cups powdered sugar
- ✓ Chopped pecans and maraschino cherries, for garnish

INSTRUCTIONS

1) Prepare Mousse: In the bowl of a mixer, whip cream cheese with the whip attachment until smooth. Add orange juice and whip until combined. Running the mixer on low, add powdered sugar. Once powdered sugar is mixed in, increase speed to medium high and beat until smooth. Fold in Cool Whip until completely mixed in. Refrigerate until you're ready to use.

2) Prepare Frosting: In the bowl of a mixer, beat cream cheese and butter until combined. Add vanilla and powdered sugar and beat on low until just combined. Increase speed to medium high and beat for about a minute, until frosting is smooth, light, and fluffy.

3) Cut cake into circles that fill fit in the jars. You can either use a round biscuit or cookie cutter, or the mouth of one of the jars you will be using.

4) Pipe or spoon a layer of mousse in the bottom of each jar. Carefully press a cake circle on top, and finish by piping or spooning frosting on top of that. Add a cherry and sprinkle with chopped pecans.

5) Place a lid on each jar and chill until ready to serve.

88. Snickers Pudding Parfaits

INGREDIENTS

- 1 box (4 serving size) instant vanilla pudding
- 1/2 cup crunchy peanut butter
- 2 boxes instant chocolate pudding
- 5 1/2 cups cold whole milk
- 2 cups heavy cream
- 4 Tablespoons powdered sugar
- 1/2 cup caramel syrup (the kind in the squirt bottle, not the kind in the jar you have to microwave)
- Snicker Bars, chopped (I used fun size ones from Halloween)

INSTRUCTIONS

1) Pour both boxes of chocolate pudding and 4 cups milk in a large bowl, and prepare according to package directions. Set in the refrigerator to chill.
2) Put the vanilla pudding mix, 1 1/2 cups milk, and the crunchy peanut butter in a medium bowl. Whisk according to package directions and place bowl in the refrigerator.
3) In the bowl of a stand mixer fitted with the whisk attachment, add the heavy cream, caramel sauce, and powdered sugar. Beat on high until thick. Stop beating as soon as it reaches the consistency of whipped cream--do NOT overbeat.
4) For best results when whipping cream, I always place my mixer bowl and whisk attachment in the freezer at least 10 minutes prior to using.

5) In small bowls, parfait glasses, or trifle bowls, layer chocolate pudding, crunchy peanut butter pudding, and more chocolate pudding. Top with caramel whipped cream, chopped Snicker bars, and a drizzle of caramel syrup.

89. Lemon Mascarpone Parfaits

INGREDIENTS
- 1 cup crushed cookies (preferably Biscoff or ginger snaps)
- 16 oz. mascarpone cheese
- 1-1/2 cups lemon curd (homemade or store-bought)
- 1 cup cool whip or creme fraiche
- 6-8 whole cookies, for garnish

INSTRUCTIONS
1) Set aside individual serving dishes or glasses for the parfaits. {The number of parfaits you make will depend on the size of the dishes/glasses used. If you use smaller glasses, you'll get about 6-8 mini parfaits.}
2) In the bowl of your mixer, beat together the mascarpone cheese and lemon curd until smooth and creamy, about 2-3 minutes.
3) Spoon 1-2 tablespoons of crushed cookies into each individual serving dish or glass.
4) Divide the lemon mascarpone filling evenly between the serving glasses, topping each layer of cookie crumbs with about 1 cup of the filling.
5) Top the lemon mascarpone layer with a dollop of cool whip or creme fraiche, and garnish with a cookie, if using.
6) Refrigerate at least 1 hour before serving, and enjoy!

90. Cinnamon Apple Pear Parfait

INGREDIENTS

- ✓ 2 small apples, peeled and diced
- ✓ 1 pear, peeled and diced
- ✓ 1 T. brown sugar
- ✓ 1/8 t. cinnamon
- ✓ pinch of salt
- ✓ 1 cup non fat plain Greek yogurt
- ✓ 1 T. honey
- ✓ 1/8 t. cinnamon

INSTRUCTIONS

1) Preheat oven to 400 degrees.
2) Line a baking sheet with foil (sprayed with cooking spray) or a silpat mat.
3) In a small bowl toss the peeled, diced apples and pear together with the brown sugar and cinnamon until everything is coated.
4) Pour the fruit onto the lined baking sheet and bake for 20 minutes.
5) When the fruit is finished roasting let it cool to room temperature or chill it in the fridge.
6) In a separate bowl whisk together the yogurt, honey, and cinnamon.
7) Take two small glasses and put a layer of fruit on the bottom and top the fruit with a couple spoonfuls of the yogurt mixture.
8) Continue to layer the fruit and yogurt ending with the fruit on top.
9) Serve immediately or cover with plastic wrap and refrigerate them until you are ready to eat.

91. Banana Coconut Cream Pie Parfaits

INGREDIENTS

- ✓ 2 cups Almond Breeze Almondmilk Coconutmilk Vanilla Unsweeteend
- ✓ 1/2 cup granulated sugar
- ✓ 3 heaping tablespoons cornstarch
- ✓ 1/4 teaspoon kosher salt
- ✓ 1 egg
- ✓ 1 1/2 teaspoons vanilla extract or vanilla bean paste
- ✓ 3/4 cup almond meal
- ✓ 1/4 cup toasted unsweetened coconut
- ✓ 1 tablespoon brown sugar
- ✓ 1/2 tablespoon coconut oil
- ✓ Pinch of salt
- ✓ 2 ripe bananas, thinly sliced

- ✓ Toasted unsweetened coconut for sprinkling on top of the parfaits
- ✓ Whipped cream

INSTRUCTIONS

1) In a medium sized saucepan over medium high heat, heat the almond/coconut milk until bubbles start to form around the edge.

2) In a medium sized bowl whisk together the sugar, cornstarch, salt, and egg until well combined.

3) Slowly pour the hot milk into the dry mixture whisking the entire time.

4) Pour the mixture back into the saucepan and continue to whisk it over medium heat until it thickens, about 4-5 minutes.

5) Once it thickens lower the heat to low and whisk for another 1-2 minutes.

6) Remove the pudding from the heat and whisk in the vanilla extract.

7) Pour the pudding back into the bowl that the dry ingredients were in and place it into an ice bath.

8) Continue to whisk the pudding every couple minutes until it has cooled completely.

9) Cover the pudding with plastic wrap, placing the plastic directly onto the pudding, and refrigerate until ready to serve.

10) In a food processor pulse together all of the ingredients for the crust until combined, don't over-pulse or you may turn it into almond butter.

11) Place about 2 tablespoons of the crust mixture into the bottom of 4 small glasses or bowls.

12) Place 4-5 banana slices on top of the crust.

13) Spoon about 3 tablespoons of the pudding on top of the bananas then repeat the process with the remaining crust, banana slices, and pudding.

14) Top the parfaits with whipped cream and more toasted coconut if desired.

92. Special K Parfait

INGREDIENTS

- Dannon Light & Fit Nonfat Vanilla Yogurt, 8 oz
- Strawberries, .5 cup sliced
- Kellogg's Special K Cereal, 1 cup

INSTRUCTIONS

1) In tall glass, layer yogurt, fruit and cereal until glass is full.
2) Top with extra fruit.
3) Serve immediately.

93. Mother's Day Spring Parfait

INGREDIENTS

- 1 tbsp custard powder
- 1 tbsp sugar
- 1/2 cup of whole milk, divided
- 1 tsp vanilla
- 1/4 tsp grated lemon zest
- 150 g fresh (or frozen, thawed, juices reserved) mango, cubed small
- 1/2 cup fresh (or frozen, thawed, juices reserved) blueberries
- 2 tbsp water
- 1 tbsp honey

- ✓ 1 tbsp brown sugar
- ✓ 1 tbsp cornstarch
- ✓ 3 tbsp cold water (or reserved fruit thawing juices)
- ✓ 1 1/4 cups rolled oats
- ✓ 3 tbsp honey
- ✓ 2 tbsp water
- ✓ 1/4 tsp vanilla
- ✓ 1 tsp canola oil (if needed, included in NI)

INSTRUCTIONS

1) Combine powder, sugar and 1 tbsp of milk to a paste in saucepan, add remaining milk and heat to just under the boil. Cook 5 minutes or until thickened, stirring, then remove from heat and let cool 2 minutes. Stir in the vanilla and lemon zest and chill before serving. Can be made 1-2 days in advance.

2) Combine the fruit, 2 tbsp water, honey and brown sugar in a small saucepan, bring to a simmer and cook 6-8 minutes, stirring frequently, until the fruit begins to break down. Whisk together cornstarch and water (or juice) in a small dish until smooth. Stir the slurry into the cooking mixture and simmer, stirring for 1-2 minutes until thick and the fruit is coated. Can be used warm over pancakes and waffles, for this parfait cool completely. Can be made up to 5 days in advance.

3) Preheat oven to 275F. Line a baking sheet with parchment. Combine all ingredients in a small mixing bowl - I find tossing and mixing by hand works best - until everything is evenly coated. Spread evenly on the lined sheet, as close to one layer as possible. Bake for 20 minutes, then rotate the pan in the oven. Bake a further 10-15 minutes, or until the oats are crispy, toasted and mostly dry. Cool completely on sheet, then stir to get the clusters. Store in an airtight tin. Can be made up to 10 days in advance.

4) Layer an even smount of custard on the bottom of each serving dish. Top with a generous amount of fruit, then add equal amounts of granola to the top of each dish. Serve immediately.

94. Amaranth Yogurt Parfait

INGREDIENTS
- ½ cup full fat fresh curd/yogurt or as required
- 1 small muskmelon/honey dew melon
- 1 medium sized ripe sweet mango
- 10-12 cashews
- 15-16 golden raisins
- 5 to 6 dry figs
- 2 tbsp amaranth seeds
- honey as required

INSTRUCTIONS
1) Heat a pan till its hot. Add 1 or 2 tbsp of the amaranth and allow them to pop with the method mentioned in the post above.
2) Remove the popped amaranth from the pan and keep aside.
3) Peel and chop the mango and the honey dew melon.
4) Roast the cashews in the same pan till golden. Keep aside.
5) Chop the dry figs and keep aside.
6) Layer the glass or individual serving bowls with 1 or 2 tbsp yogurt.
7) Drizzle ½ to 1 tsp honey or as required on the yogurt.
8) Then make a layer of the fruits.
9) Add the dry fruits and again drizzle honey.
10) Layer with some of the popped amaranth.
11) Then again drizzle with some honey. Repeat the same layers.
12) Serve the amaranth yogurt parfait immediately.

95. Sweet and Toasty Parfait

Parfaits don't only have to be made with yogurt. Make a sweet and delicious parfait using s'mores <u>ingredients</u> by placing graham crackers in a small Mason jar with chocolate pudding and toasted marshmallows — yum!

INSTRUCTIONS

1) <u>Place 3 marshmallows on a parchment-lined baking sheet and broil on high for 1 minute. Place 3 tablespoons of graham cracker crumbs in an 8 ounce glass or jar. Add 1/4 cup chocolate pudding and top with the marshmallows.</u>

96. Walnut Ginger Granola Parfait

INGREDIENTS
- 4 Cups old-fashioned rolled oats
- 1 1/2 Cup chopped walnuts
- 1 Teaspoon ground ginger
- 1/4 Teaspoon sea salt
- 1/4 Cup sunflower oil
- 1/2 Cup agave nectar or maple syrup
- 2 egg whites, whipped until light and frothy
- 1 Cup crystallized ginger, finely chopped
- Edible flowers such as pansies, geraniums, or marigolds, for garnish
- 1-2 Cup Greek yogurt, for parfait

INSTRUCTIONS
1) Preheat the oven to 325 degrees.
2) Combine thte oats, chopped nuts, ground ginger, and sea salt in a large bowl. Toss well so that the ingredients are well mixed. Pour the oil into the bowl, following by the agave nectar. Mix well with a spatula until all of the ingredients are combined.
3) Add the whipped egg whites to the bowl and toss the mixture to coat.
4) Spread the granola onto a baking sheet. Bake until golden brown, approximately 30 minutes. Make sure to toss granola every 8-10 minutes during the baking process to evenly cook.
5) Remove from the oven and sprinkle the crystallized ginger over the hot granola. Stir quickly then allow granola to cool completely for several hours.
6) Spoon the Greek yogurt into a glass parfait cup. Top with the granola and garnish with an edible flower.

97. Tropical "Candy Corn" Protein Parfait

INGREDIENTS

- ✓ 1 Cup frozen pineapple
- ✓ 1 Cup frozen mango
- ✓ 1/2 Cup water
- ✓ 1 Tablespoon yogurt of choice
- ✓ 1 serving vanilla protein powder, such as ALOHA Vanilla Protein
- ✓ 2 Teaspoons coconut, such as ALOHA Coconut
- ✓ 1/2 Tablespoon chopped fresh ginger (optional)
- ✓ 1 Tablespoon fresh lemon juice (optional)

INSTRUCTIONS

1) Add the pineapple and 1/4 cup water to a blender or food processor; if you want a zestier parfait, add the ginger and lemon as well. Blend well and add the purée to a clear glass. For best results, place it in the freezer while you prepare the rest of the parfait.

2) Blend the mango and 1/4 cup water. Remove the pineapple from the freezer and pour the mango on top of it. Again, place it in your freezer.

3) Mix your yogurt, ALOHA Protein, and ALOHA Coconut in a bowl. Remove your parfait from the freezer and add the protein yogurt on top. Enjoy!

98. Spiked Peppermint Brownie Parfait

INGREDIENTS

- 1 Fiber One 90 calorie peppermint fudge brownie
- 3 tbsp. light vanilla yogurt
- 1 tsp. Irish cream liqueur
- 1/4 tsp. red color sugar

INSTRUCTIONS

1) Dip the rim of a mini martini glass in yogurt and colored sugar. Stir Irish cream liquer into vanilla yogurt and spoon into the glass. Top with a brownie that has been cut into 4 pieces.

99. Rainbow Dessert Parfaits

INGREDIENTS

- 2 (6-count) boxes Fiber One 90 Calorie Lemon Bar
- 1 container Yoplait Fat Free red raspberry yogurt
- 1 container Yoplait Light orange crème yogurt
- 1 container Yoplait Light Fat Free lemon cream pie yogurt
- 1 container Yoplait Light Fat Free Key lime pie yogurt
- 1 container Yoplait Original 99% Fat Free Piña Colada Yogurt
- 1 container Yoplait Light Fat Free blueberry patch yogurt
- 4 cups whipped topping, divided
- Betty Crocker gel food colors: neon pink, neon orange, yellow, neon green, blue, and neon purple
- Bubble gum balls (red, orange, yellow, green, blue, purple—optional)

INSTRUCTIONS

1) Open each lemon bar and crumble into a large bowl. Set aside.
2) In a small bowl, whisk together the container of raspberry yogurt with 3/4 cup whipped topping until fluffy. Tint red. Repeat until each container of yogurt has been whisked together with whipped topping and gel food color: orange creme with orange, lemon with yellow, lime with green, pina colada with blue, and blueberry with purple. Spoon each colored yogurt whip into separate pastry bags.
3) Place 1 tablespoon of lemon-bar crumble into the bottom of six martini glasses. Snip a 3/4-inch opening in the tip of each pastry bag. Pipe a layer of colored yogurt whip on top (one color for each glass), add another 3 tablespoons of lemon-bar crumble, and finish with a swirl of yogurt whip on top. Garnish with color-coordinating bubble gum balls. Refrigerate until ready to serve. Enjoy!

100. Sweetheart Strawberry Yogurt Parfaits

INGREDIENTS

- ✓ 1/2 cup white chocolate chips
- ✓ 1 tablespoon honey
- ✓ Mini heart sprinkles
- ✓ 2 (6 oz) containers of Yoplait Original strawberry yogurt
- ✓ 1/2 cup frozen whipped topping

INSTRUCTIONS

1) Melt your white chocolate chips in the microwave at 50% power in 15 second intervals, stirring with a completely dry utensil. Do not let water come into contact with the chocolate or it will seize. Stir and heat until the chocolate is smooth and melted.

2) Place the white chocolate into a piping back or a plastic zipper bag and snip off a small corner of the bag. Pipe out 4 heart shapes onto parchment or wax paper. Let dry completely.

3) Place the mini parfait glass upside down into a small dish with the honey. Make sure the rim of the glass is coated. Immediately dip the honey-coated glass rim into a small dish filled with the mini heart sprinkles.

4) Carefully spoon a small amount of the strawberry yogurt into the mini parfait glass. Do the same with the frozen whipped topping, alternating layers until you end with the frozen whipped topping.

5) Top your parfait with a white chocolate heart.

Made in the USA
Monee, IL
08 September 2023

42370696R00069